Susie C. (Susie Champney) Clark

The round Trip: from the Hub to the Golden Gate

Susie C. (Susie Champney) Clark

The round Trip: from the Hub to the Golden Gate

ISBN/EAN: 9783743313248

Manufactured in Europe, USA, Canada, Australia, Japa

Cover: Foto ©Andreas Hilbeck / pixelio.de

Manufactured and distributed by brebook publishing software (www.brebook.com)

Susie C. (Susie Champney) Clark

The round Trip: from the Hub to the Golden Gate

THE ROUND TRIP

FROM THE HUB

TO

THE GOLDEN GATE

BY

SUSIE C. CLARK

AUTHOR OF "A LOOK UPWARD" "TO BEAR WITNESS" ETC.

BOSTON MDCCCXC
LEE AND SHEPARD PUBLISHERS
10 MILK STREET NEXT "THE OLD SOUTH MEETING HOUSE"
NEW YORK CHARLES T. DILLINGHAM
718 AND 720 BROADWAY

COPYRIGHT, 1890, BY SUSIE C. CLARK

THE ROUND TRIP

PRESS OF
AMERICAN PRINTING AND ENGRAVING CO.
50 ARCH STREET, BOSTON

CONTENTS

CHAPTER		PAGE
I.	Departure	5
II.	Through Canada to Chicago	10
III.	Across the Plains to Santa Fe	15
IV.	Over the Desert to Paradise	20
V.	Pasadena	24
VI.	Psaadena — Its Environs	30
VII.	Los Angeles — Santa Monica	36
VIII.	Santa Barbara	41
IX.	Riverside	48
X.	San Diego	54
XI.	En Route	62
XII.	San Francisco	71
XIII.	Oakland	81
XIV.	The Rainy Season	87
XV.	Sonoma County	93
XVI.	The Lick Observatory	99
XVII.	Santa Cruz — Monterey	111
XVIII.	To the Yo Semite	119
XIX.	In the Valley	132
XX.	Homeward Bound	144
XXI.	Salt Lake City	153
XXII.	The Scenic Route	163
XXIII.	How We Spent Memorial Day	172
XXIV.	The Home Stretch	183

THE ROUND TRIP

CHAPTER I

DEPARTURE

A CERTAIN dear little lady, who was so unfortunate (though she might not agree with our representation of the case) as to marry a naval officer, and consequently spent her days migrating from one port to another, on the eastern, western, or southern shores of our republic, according to the transient location of her husband's ship, that she might gain occasional glimpses of the glittering shoulder-straps and brass buttons of her truant lord, once gave to us as her profound conviction, this maxim: "If you want to be uncomfortable — *travel!*"

We could not gainsay her then, but can see plainly enough now, that the confession ranked her as one who has never placed herself under the espionage of those successful managers, Messrs. Raymond and Whitcomb, who make of travelling a science and an art, whose trains furnish every feature of a home but its usual stationary quality, and this is not always one to be desired. Human as well as vegetable growth is often encouraged by the process of transplanting, and removal in this instance is accomplished so deftly, skillfully and delightfully that the wrench of leaving one's native soil is scarcely felt, even though the new habitat is the width of a continent distant, and active life is resumed in a new world, a new climate, and under sunnier skies than the rockbound coast of dear old New England affords.

But California is much nearer Boston than it was in '49. The journey thither is hardly now considered much of a trip. The Raymonds certainly leave you no anxiety in regard to it, and little to do but to fold your arms and be taken care of. The start is made from the station at the foot of Causeway street, which structure seems a relic of some feudal age, and makes a refreshing oasis to the artistic eye amid the square, stiff, red walls of its democratic surroundings. Its stern exterior and battlemented towers, with its moat and draw-bridge might have served as a castle of the Norman conqueror, although his outposts of defence were not adorned by such mazy network of electric wires.

The Fitchburg's straight and narrow path runs through classic ground; Cambridge, earliest home of letters, name indissolubly connected with memories of Longfellow, Agassiz, Holmes, Gray, and a score of lesser lights, Cambridge, which also holds the deserted hearthstone, and the friends who waft, we know, a strong God-speed; Belmont, long the home of Howells; Waverley, whose ancient oaks and Beaver brook are immortalized in Lowell's limpid verse; Waltham, making time for half the world; and Concord,

> "Where first th' embattled farmers stood,
> And fired the shot heard round the world,'

the opening of that history, written in the nation's heart-blood, whose second chapter is marked by the granite shaft which rises from Charlestown's hill. Fair Walden's placid wave recalls the gentle soul who built a lodge upon its shore and learned his lessons in Nature's school. The tall hemlocks and whispering pines that fringe its banks, chant no requiem in our ears for the departed great — Emerson and Hawthorne, Thoreau and Alcott — whose fellowship they have enjoyed, but murmur thanks that some there are in every age who understand their song and interpret all their mystic lore in words that our duller ears can reach.

Darkness begins to settle as we enter the lovely Deerfield valley, veiling the winding river and diversity of hill and glen, the grace of outline and brilliancy of autumnal foliage. But here the courteous conductor invites us to the dining car, where attentive liveried waiters present us with a *menu* that might well engage the attention of the most fastidious epicure.

Later on, our commodious section is converted into a tempting couch, and just as we are composing ourselves to rest thereon, no less secure in the protection which never faileth than we would be in the familiar home-nest, a parting glance of inquiry toward the outside world reveals a giant mountain wall directly athwart our path. Even our iron horse pauses for the moment, as if dismayed, then with two or three exultant neighs plunges straight onward, for the giant opes his heart and lets us in. Mind has conquered matter, as it always must, being its parent. Ten minutes or more are required for the gloomy passage, but what do those ten minutes represent? What years of patient toil, and herculean obstacles overcome,

> "Ere first the locomotive wheels
> Rolled thro' the Hoosac tunnel bore."

First projected in 1825, the tunnel was discussed in legislative halls for a quarter of a century, was laid repeatedly on the table and partially forgotten, only to be revived, for the matter — like Banquo's ghost — would not down. A royal road to the West was the coming need, and in 1851 the work was begun. The State appropriated $2,000,000, but the actual expense was ten times that amount, besides the cost of many brave souls who here found sepulchre.

After bustling, noisy North Adams, with its ever clanging bells, has been left behind, the silence of slumber reigns in our narrow borders, while with ever increasing pace we speed onwards, finding ourselves at early dawn, or late starlight, in the region between Syracuse and pretty Rochester, a country whose lazy canal-boats mock the demands of our modern commerce, and where the sun rises gloriously in the northwest, or so it seemed from the sightly observatory of a Pullman pillow.

And the evening and the morning were the first day!

CHAPTER II

THROUGH CANADA TO CHICAGO

IT has been said that the Raymonds always give their patrons more than they agree to, and therefore their California excursionists were not surprised on the second day out to be taken through London and Paris before proceeding on their American tour. But travelling in foreign countries has its disadvantages. For instance, we are nothing if not literary. Correspondence with friends at home is a trade well followed in our midst, and at every stopping place mail boxes are eagerly sought for, in which to deposit these friendly greetings. At Hamilton, Canada, a most enticing letter-box was seen, and a lady of the party who shall be nameless, was delegated to skip across the intervening tracks with a freight of postal cards. On the way thither, the thought that she was in Canada bid her pause, but recalling that the same cards when mailed in Boston reached Canada in safety she thought it a poor rule that would not work both ways, so she slammed the iron lid sharply down on the vanished treasures only to hear at her elbow:

"They won't go!"

"Won't go? And why?"

Explanations followed, and at this juncture a sleepy Canadian shuffled up and offered to put extra stamps on the whole batch when the collector should arrive. Gratefully, the lady took from her purse some brand new pennies, bright and glittering as gold pieces, but the man removed neither hand from his pocket to receive the same. Then she tried him on some this-year nickels, but with an extra puff of his old clay pipe he grunted out:

"They're no use to me."

Growing exasperated, she next sought for dimes, ten cent's worth of pure silver the world over, but the provoking individual was still unmoved. Here the incensed American citizen made a stand. She assured him in good strong English, which at least he did have the grace to take, that his miserable Canadian dimes were in very bad odor with us; the Post Offices wouldn't take them, the West End conductors refused to look at them, and that her dimes were the only legitimate dimes in good and regular standing, but just here the courteous agent of the party, who unlike the average policeman, *is* always round when wanted, appeared on the scene and straightened out the matter beautifully.

At twilight of our long Canadian day we were ferried across the St. Clair river to Michigan, and the stars and stripes once more waved over the brave and the free. We even fancied that the American bird clapped his wings and crowed with especial zest and fervor upon our entrance next morning into boisterous, rampant Chicago.

And where in all this fair land is there anything just like Chicago—so masterful, rich and proud—the young Leviathan of the West? Rising from her cleansing fires in massive, stately grandeur, she uses the heroic scale of measurement in her every expression of life. She builds her warehouses by the mile, her palaces cover leagues. She is already making confident preparation, to hold here the World's Fair of 1892. For, she reasons, what would the trans-atlantic visitor know of the wondrous length and breadth of our country if he landed in New York, and saw only the Exposition?

The beautiful Lincoln Park, with its Lake boulevard, hopes to add ere that date still another to its many attractions in an artificial drive across the water, 800 feet from shore, parallel with the Park. Wealth is plentiful, merchants princely, and Western hearts generous. A new statue was placed in the Park, a week ago, a bronze figure of De La Salle, a discoverer of hardly less note than Columbus, for did he not discover Chicago? It is supposed that this brave French explorer was the first white man to set his foot, 209 years ago, upon the soil now covered by the great metropolis, or in the Indian village which then occupied its site.

The Park visitor can hardly fail to visit the tank of sea-lions, as his attention is drawn thither by the constant, hideous barking noise with which these unpleasant, slimy creatures seek to relieve their rudimentary minds. One cannot help the query *cui bono* while gazing on these strange useless connecting links in the great chain of life. It is as if Nature paused, in sportive mood, while ascending the ladder of creation to use up waste material, the refuse of more decided types, of fish, and dog and ape. The imprisoned germ of a soul which vitalizes the shapeless lump we call sea-lion is certainly very restive under its present imperfect expression. It writhes uncomfortably, and yearns impatiently for its next higher transmigration, which, we know, will surely come.

Chicago's Public Library occupies commodious quarters on the top floor of the city's magnificent Court House, with many stations in various other districts. The streets of Chicago are noticeably more uncleanly and filled with refuse than the thoroughfares of a certain thrifty New England city we could mention, but the visitor who dared to comment on this state of affairs was assured with considerable hauteur that there is so much more business done here than in Boston that it would be impossible to keep the streets so tidy. Dear, insignificant little Boston! Though so far away, we love her still.

CHAPTER III

ACROSS THE PLAINS TO SANTA FE

FROM Chicago, our course lies straight as the crow flies across the prairie State of Illinois and through its acres upon acres of corn fields, to Rock Island and the Mississippi. This noble river, broad, placid and beautiful, is crossed at sunset, while it still reflects the sky's warm glow in its every ripple. Its sister river, the Missouri, reached at daybreak the next morning, is more churlish. Yellow, tawny and turbulent, she veils her unloveliness with a fog so dense that her width can hardly be discerned from the height of the bridge, and Kansas City on its rugged bluffs is entirely blotted out. Indeed the precipitous heights on which the place seems perched, are so exaggerated by this deceptive haze that we now credit the legend of a cow who here fell out of a pasture and broke her neck.

From this point onward we enter upon the plains and cross many leagues of level, unfertile, but to unaccustomed eyes, most interesting stretch of country. Its chief vegetation consists of clumps of sage brush and huge cacti, bristling with light yellow blossoms, its chief inhabitants prairie-dogs, so-called, though the term seems a misnomer, for the little creatures hop like rabbits, are nearer the color of rats, and not so large as a gray-squirrel. The little conical-shaped mounds which form their dwellings (though hardly higher than the ant-hills in this strange land), form prominent features in the landscape, showing a singular absence of the sense of danger, or need of protection, common to all animals in their native state.

Herds of cattle are occasionally seen, though what they can find on this yellowish grey soil by which to support life is a mystery. That some have failed in the struggle for existence, bleached bones and skeletons along our path sadly testify. A stray emigrant train, drawn by patient oxen, threads tediously the old Indian trail, and in the distance, on our Western boundary, is a background of snow-capped mountains, the Spanish peaks, the Custar range, and at Trinidad the adjacent and awe-inspiring Fisher's Peak. It seems a few rods away, but we are assured it is 14 miles distant by actual measurement, such is the deceptive brilliancy of this glorious air. We are favored with many different views of this Gibraltar-like fortress as we skirt its borders, and, dividing our attention on the other side is another lofty eminence, surmounted by a monument, and known as Simpson's Rest, for here one of the old pioneers was buried at his earnest request. Later in the day, we approach Wagon Mound, a summit of solid rock, up which the American soldiers with ropes once dragged their provision wagons when surrounded by Mexicans, only to meet slow starvation, surrender and pitiless massacre. Every point of interest in our course is carefully emphasized by our ever vigilant porter, who seems to be a walking cyclopædia of information, whose good nature is boundless, and whose patience threatens to eclipse that of Job, for did that ancient worthy ever stand the exacting test of a sleeping car?

Then, leaving these heights, we ride for miles and yet other miles, without a tree or rock in sight, the land level as if it had been rolled, until it reaches and touches the distant sky. Just before twilight we reach Las Vegas Hot Springs, and here we become still further the recipients of the Raymond generosity, for a telegram from Boston directs that after spending a few hours at the Springs, (to test the boiling waters and climb to the turret of the pretty hotel, a veritable Hall of Montezuma, to enjoy the charming view), we are to be treated to a side trip not down in the bill, and move on during the night to Santa Fé, that we may spend Sunday in that quaint old town, the oldest in the country, for it ante-dates St. Augustine by some years, the Spaniards finding a settlement here in 1542, and calling the people pueblos, or villagers, to distinguish them from the native tribes.

Who can ever forget a Sabbath spent in Santa Fé? Even now in its freshness it seems like an impossible dream of the middle ages. We were first invited to Fort Marcy at 9, to witness Guard Mount (whatever that is), and inspection of guns, the soldier who owned the cleanest one being appointed boss of the squad for the day. (This is not a strict quotation from Hardee.) A very fine band is stationed here, and gave excellent selections of sacred music, greatly appreciated by their impromptu audience.

We next visit the Cathedral at the hour of mass, feeling as if we belonged to another race than that of the devout worshippers here assembled, while still realizing that we are all children of the same Infinite Father. The women all wore black shawls over their heads, gathered under the chin with a peculiar grasp of the left hand. We then seek the little Presbyterian church established here and attend its service, after which we stroll about the narrow streets, designed only for donkey travel, or *burros*, as the tough little creatures are called, these primitive thoroughfares boasting no sidewalks but are lined with low adobe houses, whose unattractive exteriors are often a mask to conceal the home within, the pleasant court-yard with its verdure, upon which the living rooms open. We look up occasionally at the stars and stripes waving over the fort to convince ourselves that the Atlantic does not roll between us and home, for the town seems like a leaf from old Spain, certainly like nothing American, or progressive.

In the *plaza*, a park in the centre of the town, stands a monument to the bravery of those soldiers who fell fighting the rebels, the only inscription which includes that word "rebel," in the country.

The Ramona school for the education of Indian children, under the auspices of the A. M. A., is located here, as also a governmental school, and the University of New Mexico. The Territorial Capitol building is very fine.

But the most interesting thing we learned at Santa Fé was that in a low building fronting on the *plaza*, erected in 1581, Gen. Lew Wallace, for some time Governor of New Mexico, penned his famous "Ben Hur." No wonder that he described Jerusalem scenery and characteristics so accurately, for its every quaint and ancient feature here abounds, even to the mountains that are round about Jerusalem, surmounted by the peak, 12,000 feet above the sea, which never, in winter or in summer, doffs its eternal crown of snow.

CHAPTER IV

OVER THE DESERT TO PARADISE

PASSING from New Mexico into Arizona during the night, the tourist opens his eyes when the next morning dawns, upon a still wider stretch of plains, on longer areas of sterile waste, until he feels ready to exclaim: "Is there no end to this country?" And yet the monotony never becomes wearisome to this merry party, who seldom fail to pour tumultuously out onto the platform of every little station where we stop to take on water or ice, and if time permits, the town is invaded, stores visited, shanties inspected that often bear signs of disproportionate size, labelled "Palace Hotel," "Big Lunch, 5 cts.," or "Aunt Hannah's Pioneer Store," this proprietress being, she affirms, a Boston lady, who having kept the store 53 years, is desirous of selling out and returning to her native city, a decision of which our Eastern capitalists on the lookout for investments, should become cognizant. Most of the towns in this far West are lighted at evening by electric lights, they have cable, or electric cars, an example which some Eastern cities have since followed.

At noon, the wild Canon Diablo is passed, an utterly barren gorge of rocks and on the iron bridge which crosses it, the train pauses a little longer than some weak nerves prefer that all may inspect this natural wonder. And now the San Francisco mountains rear their heads across our horizon, and the scene grows wilder. Flag-Staff is passed (so-called because on an adjacent peak, Gen. Fremont hoisted the American flag), and here also is a quarry of red stone used by Los Angeles builders. Then for some time we wind around Williams' Mountain, a grand height, with the tombstone to the old pioneer whose name it bears, plainly visible on its summit, and just before nightfall we thread our narrow, tortuous course around Johnson's canon, a dangerous chasm, whose precipitous depths, and jagged outlines, as viewed from our narrow perch on the mountain's side, we are glad to leave behind.

"The Needles," a narrow pass, which with the Colorado river forms the boundary line between Arizona and California are passed at midnight, together with the eastern portion of the Mojave desert, but there is desert enough to hold out into another day, and still wider, sandy, barren, alkaline plains greet our waking eyes, salt lying in places white as a hoar frost, the only attempt at vegetation being occasional clumps of low bushes of dusty-miller white, and others of a waxy livid green, forming a most effective contrast. Beauty never forgets her earth-child anywhere, under any circumstances. But in the desert, we sympathize with the pauper child who exclaimed on first viewing the ocean: "I niver saw enough of anything at onct, before." We begin to speculate as to the possibility of a terminus to this road. Two straight parallel lines, we recall, never meet at any given point, and the iron rails we tread are of this description.

But sterility reigns only without. Far too regularly the announcement is made that "Lunch," or "Dinner is now ready in the dining-car"; a summons often greeted with a look of comical dismay that expresses: "have we got to go through that ordeal so soon again?" For the presiding genii of that dining-car might well be arrested for cruelty to animals, so abundantly do they provide the choicest viands to this indolent, un-exercised, over-fed, pampered freight of live-stock.

At noon we begin our ascent of the Sierra Madre range of mountains, rising 215 feet to the mile amid the sublimest scenery on every side, until we reach at the summit, Cajone Pass, which is grand beyond description, and begin our descent toward the San Bernardino valley, or as some one calls it—God's own country. As we proceed, new growths excite our surprise and wonder; yucca palms as large as good-sized apple trees, the prickly-pear cactus of immense size, bearing a fruitage of pears, which are here sent to market; later on, as we approach civilization, plumes of pampas-grass, century plants that have blossomed and still bear aloft their huge crests, 60 to 80 feet high, with many new flowers and plants whose names we have yet to learn.

Speculation has been rife all day as to what time we shall "get in," as if we were on shipboard in a trackless waste of water, instead of an ocean of land; the passage of an eastward-bound overland train is calculated upon, as to what time it left Los Angeles, and now the hour of separation for this jolly family approaches. Maps and chattels are collected, autographs exchanged, farewells are waved to a carload of tourists that leaves us for the Redlands, a fruit-bearing district, of whose fertility and rapid growth we have heard such glowing accounts from some of its residents, our pleasant travelling companions, most of them New England people of sterling worth; we also take leave of another coterie, who branch off into the Pomona valley, and at dusk, we too alight upon "the crown of all the valley," fair, unrivalled Pasadena.

CHAPTER V

PASADENA

CALIFORNIA is not all a Paradise, for we have traversed miles of dreary, barren waste within her borders, but if there is an Edenic garden on earth, one fit for the occupancy of the primeval pair, that spot is Pasadena. It is true we know not what awaits us in other portions of this Golden State, but we are constantly meeting people who having tried a residence in all other localities, return delightedly to this beautiful San Gabriel valley.

Along its northern borders stretches the Sierra Madre range of mountains, a barrier that effectually protects the city nestling at its feet from every rude, cold blast, and adds to it yet another blessing, that of pure water, the principal supply coming from Devil's Gate, though one would naturally look for fire from this source rather than cooling springs. The charm also of grandeur and sublimity, Pasadena by this proximity, does not lack. With David, we "lift our eyes unto the hills," for we cannot help it. They entice us, they appal us, they command our reverence, they invite our ever changing admiration by their shifting phases. Severe in outline, seamed with gorges, and chasms, producing thus a strange wrinkled effect as if some Titan hand held aloft a vast drapery that thence fell naturally in seam, and crease, and fold; almost barren of vegetation, seemingly unwooded, though we are assured that impenetrable forests exist in some of their wildest depths, but in compensation for this softening charm of New England hills, the loftier Sierras veil themselves in shadowy mists and vapors, they play hide seek with fleecy clouds, that drift across their breasts and lurk in their deep valleys, while still rearing aloft their hoary heads into the clear blue ether which envelopes them with a light that was never seen before on sea or land, while grander than all, old "Baldy" smiles down on the fertile valley from his realm of snow. Cruel mothers (madres), these jagged peaks have proved to many venturesome climbers, nearly a dozen people having perished here in the last three years, in sight of home, being lured into some chasm, or death-trap, from which there was no escape.

On a lofty summit of the range, known as Wilson's Peak, has been recently established the Southern Pacific Observatory, for which Messrs. Alvan Clark and Sons, are manufacturing what it is expected will prove the largest lens in the world.

Sixteen years ago last summer (in 1873), a little colony from Indiana emigrated westward to select a location for a new home in the then barren wilds of California. Arriving in Los Angeles in August, they thoroughly examined localities in San Diego and San Bernardino counties, but finally selected the present site of Pasadena as offering the greatest advantages of soil, water and scenery, and the world now applauds the wisdom of their choice. But when our pioneers first settled here, in all this region now teeming with fertility and luxuriance of fruitful growth on every hand, not a tree existed, save two or three live-oaks, and the whole plateau was one sheet of flame under the reign of the golden poppy, so common in California.

When a name for the little colony was sought, that of Indianola was discussed as indicative of its origin, but to the late Dr. T. B. Elliot is due the suggestion of Pasadena, an Iroquois word signifying the "Crown of the Valley," a title which by every right it holds.

With a rapidity of cultivation almost incredible to Eastern experience, the town is now one vast garden and orange grove, though this latter designation seems to us a misnomer. A "grove" to New England ears suggests a spontaneous growth of tallish trees which cast a shade upon the greensward, or tangled underbrush beneath. There is no shade in an orange orchard, and if there were, we could not walk therein, for no grass is allowed to grow, as in our apple orchards. The ground is kept constantly plowed and irrigated. The trees, set twenty to thirty feet apart, diamond-wise, are short and bushy, and very handsome. Their foliage of dark rich glossy green is tipped on all out-lying branches with a new growth of lightest marine green, producing a weird effect of contrast, and on these showy banners, white fragrant blossoms appear, while at the same time, hanging thickly in the dense heart of the tree is the golden ripening fruit, making one of the most beautiful, picturesque objects that Nature, even in this her most lavish workshop, can produce.

The eucalyptus tree, a native of Australia, abounds here, and is a rapid grower, although it reveals much indecision of purpose, as to whether it will prove itself first cousin to the willow or the poplar, two and often three distinct types of leaves, in shape and color, appearing on the same tree. It invariably begins existence in a different frame of mind from that which maturer reflection dictates.

And who shall describe that graceful, airy growth, that sensitive plant aspiring skyward, known as the pepper-tree? Each leaf a pendant fern, of the most delicate spring green, massed together in luxuriant clusters, and drooping a little like the weeping-willow though not so much, while hanging from every finger-tip are long graceful racemes of small crimson berries, of green ones just forming, or of delicate sprays of greenish-white blossoms, all on dress-parade at once, and emitting a spicy, pungent odor that makes a walk beneath their shade most agreeable. Marengo avenue in this city, as well as many other pleasant drives, are lined with these beautiful pepper-trees of such advanced growth that their branches meet in a graceful arch over the street, which forms a vista in perspective almost too weird in its loveliness to belong to this mundane sphere.

Miles of low cypress hedge, that lends itself so readily to any device of the pruner's knife, to arches, gateposts surmounted by urns, vases, or baskets with graceful handles, adorn or enclose handsome residences everywhere. And of the flowers one hesitates to speak unless the pen could be dipped in rainbow dye. Climatic conditions being here so perfect and so exceptional, only the lightest frost two or three times a year being ever experienced, no fires necessary in an ordinary season, even at Christmas, open doors and seats on the veranda being enjoyable save at evening or early morn, plants of all kinds have nothing else to do but grow without ceasing, missing thus the customary experience of their Eastern sisters who are seized by the nape of their slender necks just as they get into the mood of growing and are hustled into a close room, stifled with foul gas, and often sit with their feet in cold water eight months out of twelve. It is a wonder that they ever reward us with fragrant blossoms.

Growing on then, year after year, it is no wonder that geraniums and rosebushes here become trees bristling with brilliant petals, that fuschias and lantanas grow beyond recognition, that arbutilons above our heads swing their myriad bright bells upon the air, that smilax spontaneously reaches the eaves, that ivy-geraniums cover stone walls, arbors, anything their delicate fingers can twine around, that heliotropes grow trunks that bid fair to rival that of an elephant, that dense flower-crowned hedges of callas mark boundary lines, that—that—in short, that Nature having lost all run of seasons, and her usual methodical habits of alternate rest and action, runs madly riot, being drunken with new wine—the wine of the elixir of life.

CHAPTER VI

PASADENA—ITS ENVIRONS

THE chief criticism we have heard of Pasadena is that there is not enough of it. But we have found it too wide in extent, its attractions too numerous to speedily exhaust. Day after day we thread its thoroughfares, or take its intersecting lines of horse or mule cars; we drive into the adjoining country, but our list of unvisited lions is still a long one. We make no allowance in our delightful excursions for unfavorable weather, since day after day the sky is as clear as if it had been swept, the sun warm as June, making outside wraps unnecessary, and yet while basking in this sunshine which knows no shadow, Pasadena reports no case of sunstroke, no mad-dogs, or thunder showers. Its people are mostly of Eastern birth and thence, it goes without saying, most intelligent, while possessing that warm, open-hearted cordiality so characteristic of this genial clime, a spirit too often crowded out by the nervous tension of our own work-a-day atmosphere.

One of the first out-lying attractions to command our attention is naturally "The Raymond," and one uses the word "command" advisedly, for it is like a city set upon a hill; it cannot be hid, cannot be forgotten, as its fine proportions are always in sight from any point. Built upon a bold promontory, evidently designed from the foundation of the world for its occupancy, an exhilarating climb or winding drive brings us to its, at present, inhospitable doors, for this grand hotel does not open until late in November, but its wide verandas, glistening in their spic-and-span attire of new paint invite the promenader to enjoy a view from every side which can hardly be surpassed in any land. And when surfeited with the grandeur that is remote, with the charm of rugged mountain and fertile valley, one turns enraptured to the beauty that is near at hand, for surrounding the hotel is a broad esplanade bordered with perpetually blooming flowers, with clambering vines that embower the entrances, with strange new foliage exciting fresh wonder and inquiry, until the luxuriance of this encircling garden ripples over its boundaries and runs down every path and avenue and rolling lawn of this green hillside. The goddess, Flora, holds royal court on this noble crest, and she drapes her myriad retinue with a thousand glorious dyes. Brilliancy, color and fragrance are everywhere at high tide.

Extending our drive beyond "The Raymond," through fertile ranches, given largely to orange, lemon and grape culture, the grapes being grown in European fashion, untrellised, and trimmed close to the ground, we soon reach the quiet little town of Alhambra, whence through a level avenue whose wide-reaching orange groves are fringed with waving pepper trees, we pass on through an almost dry river bed to the old San Gabriel Mission, the fourth established in Upper California (in 1771) by the Franciscan fathers, when banished from Spanish provinces. The present building, the third one erected here, is a long narrow structure of massive stone walls adobe-covered, with ten buttresses of brick, being intended for defense as well as worship, with a quaint bell-tower, and stairway of brick on the outside leading to the choir gallery. The windows are few and small, and placed very near the roof. An unlaundered, but very intelligent priest showed us through the interior which is adorned with full length portraits of the apostles, "genuine Murillos" (so he said), every one of them, painted by the artist as models, not as church property, and donated from the royal galleries at Madrid by Ferdinand and Isabella, (though not delivered till the reign of Charles V.), for the express purpose of assisting in the conversion of the wild Indian tribes through object lessons that could appeal to the eye.

The little Mexican village of San Gabriel is a most uncanny place. One breathes more freely when its one narrow street with its encroaching low adobe huts, has been passed. Its swarthy inhabitants have no vocabulary in common with our own save the one word "Meeshun," and a twitch of the arm in the right direction. We know they are the very same who helped to fell the timber when the sanctuary was built, for nothing ever could change here. The place was born old, so old that Cain might have found his wife in this locality.

A most interesting place to visit, at the other side of Pasadena, is the Ostrich farm, this "handsome" climate proving favorable to their successful culture. Three birds have been raised here from babyhood that are now fourteen months old and seven or eight feet high; the rest of the brood are Australian emigrants and can rest their chins on a nine foot pole, although but four years old, and no ostrich reaches his full growth till he attains the age of seven years. Strange ballet-dancer kind of a bird, as awkward in pose as a novice in her first tights, and yet moving with a certain majestic dignity of bearing that is "very like" a camel. The carriage of the long ungainly neck also, and the construction of the foot reveals this early companionship of the desert. How interesting are these connecting links in the great chain of life, links forged by the marvellous wisdom and diversity of the Creative Mind.

The ostrich has a clear liquid dark eye, as large as a calf's though with far more expression, which displays a peculiar scintillating flash; he has a broad flat head, a beak of generous proportions, short tongue and no teeth, and when a dozen pair of these piercing eyes, from the top of long, swaying, animated lamp-wicks hover in the air above and around you, or examine your hat-trimming as well as your hands for stray kernels of corn, the effect is rather startling. It is likewise most amusing to see them fill their mouths with water from the tank, then slowly raise their heads to allow it to run down the yard or more of gullet, its passage being plainly visible to the attentive observer. What would not the gourmand give for an organ of taste thus elongated?

Feeling doubtless that they were on exhibition, with their reputation at stake, a few of the birds showed their paces, flapped their wings, and executed a *pas seul*, with a strange mixture of awkwardness and grace that was suggestive of nothing more than Dixie as "The Flower Girl."

The kindly old gentleman who has the troupe in charge gave much valuable information concerning the birds, and corrected many mistaken opinions regarding them. They are plucked of their feathers about twice a year, or once in seven months, they lay about ten or twelve eggs in a season, which are invariably hatched by the sun shining upon their sand covered nests, as the birds rarely sit upon them. They are moreover, staunch metaphysicians, for they are never ill, and no disease ever attacks them. Their only weakness is a sensible preference for hot weather. If exposed to cold, they are simply found dead the next morning. They make no fuss about it, but quietly step out in search of a warmer clime.

No letter from Pasadena ever omits to extol this locality as a health resort. The present notice must therefore remain incomplete, for we who are enfranchised from bondage to the flesh, whose real habitat is the realm of spirit, recognize no East or West, no favorable or unfavorable physical conditions, being freed therefrom, and dwelling, in any land, "forever with the Lord" of all health and wholeness.

CHAPTER VII

LOS ANGELES—SANTA MONICA

IN the early and prosperous days of the Spanish Mission in California, soldiers were stationed at the various sanctuaries whose service it was to forcibly capture converts from the native tribes and awe them into submission, indeed it is recorded of one worthy father, who was very skillful in the use of the lasso, that "riding at full gallop into an Indian village, he would select his man as a slave-driver would his human chattel, he would lasso him, drag him to the Mission, tie him up and whip him into subjection, baptize him, Christianize him (?) and set him to work, all within the space of one hour; then away for another, without rest, *such was his zeal for the conversion of infidels.*"

What wonder that such "conversions" resulted in the degradation and ultimate extinction of these tribes, for, savage foes as they proved to other assailants, they strangely enough made little resistance to these peremptory measures of the holy fathers. Superstition holds such potent sway over the untutored mind.

Eventually it became necessary to provide some place of residence where the Mission soldiers who had so valiantly served their time, and who still desired to remain in this country, might retire with their families. For this purpose an order dated at San Gabriel Mission, August 26, 1781, was issued by the Governor of California — Felipe de Neve — directing the establishment of a pueblo, or town, upon the site lately occupied by the Indian village, Yang-na. This new town was to be under the especial patronage and fostering protection of "Our Lady, the Queen of the Angels," and to be known by her name, *La Pueblo de la Reina de los Angeles*, a title since shortened to the City of the Angels, or Los Angeles.

Situated in a level plain of wide extent, with high mountain ranges at her back, and an ocean at her feet, while on either hand stretches the most extensive fruit-bearing country in the world, how could this fair city fail to thrive and flourish and grow as if indeed all good angels smiled upon her? She numbers to-day 80,000 inhabitants, and her miles of broad level avenues are filled with fine buildings and noble residences that might serve as architectural models, including a City Hall and Post Office of which she may well be proud; they abound with granite blocks, hotels and stores stocked as choicely as the emporiums of our Eastern merchants, indeed we have seldom visited a more enterprising, stirring, energetic, and wide-awake city. It seems destined to become the second metropolis of this extensive coast, and being situated 500 miles nearer the tropics than San Francisco, in a climate and amid natural surroundings that are faultless, it must remain a favorite place of residence.

It uses the adjacent port of San Pedro for its already extensive commerce with Alaska, Mexico, and the islands of the sea, but a favorite beach-resort, thirteen miles distant, is Santa Monica, where an enjoyable day can be spent. It was here that we first sighted the broad Pacific. Balboa must look to his laurels, we too have discovered it. And it is like the Atlantic as are two halves of an orange. There is the same uneasy restlessness, and tumultuous heaving and throbbing of its mighty heart, the same ceaseless moan and sob and wail, the embodiment of everything that is sad, dreary, cruel, and pitiless, its *miserere* possibly for the many brave souls it has dragged down and crushed with greedy embrace. Obedient to the same attractions, paying court to the same fickle lunar dame, whether in coquettish mood she veils her face or illuminates these watery depths with the broad fulness of her radiant beams, the Pacific, like her ocean twin, beats time in regular rhythm to the anthem of the universe, with her advancing and retreating tides that roll in white-teethed breakers on the same sandy floor, or chase the receding feet that venture too boldly upon their domain.

But looking landward we at last mark a difference. The Nantaskets and Reveres of our Atlantic coast boast no mountains like this Santa Monica range which runs down one arm of the little bay quite to the water's edge. Their sweet breath likewise fills all the air. The briny, fishy odor which our olfactories can recall is to a landsman most blessedly conspicuous by its absence. The usual barren waste of beach-resorts, their scanty verdure, the puny spindling trees that struggle bravely to eke out a half-existence are here replaced by an adjacent garden whose boundary hedges are a thick mass of blooming Marguerites, whose taller growths are date-palms, banana trees, and magnolias bearing their huge white waxen flowers upturned to the sun, inviting the bees, the butterflies, and humming-birds to bathe, at will, in their chalices of fragrant nectar.

Shells of new varieties abound here, and there is one other oddity noticeable. Old Sol has lost his bearings, like everything else, in this land of topsy-turvy. We have been accustomed, in regarding the ocean at mid-day, to have the sun and the long lane of light which he casts upon the wave, and which every separate ripple delights to catch a little of and run away with, on our *right* hand. Here he had the effrontery, as we face the Pacific, to offend our sense of fitness by pouring forth all his glory upon our *left* hand, and seems to guide his course directly toward the East. If we turn about and get *him* in the right quarter of the heavens, the ocean is *behind* us ; our mariner's compass is de-polarized, and at last we realize that we have indeed crossed the continent.

The little town of Santa Monica close by, boasts a pleasant park, an extensive ostrich farm, and three miles away in a verdant plain, occupying three spacious red-roofed buildings, is the Soldiers' Home, whose inmates have so dearly bought the comforts they now enjoy. A farmer whom we pass is ploughing with three mules abreast, a large blue heron flies startled from a reedy swamp, strange looking creature with his long legs and bill to float in the air, other unfamiliar voices warble in our ears, mocking-birds call to us from their leaf-embowered nests, while warm, fragrance-laden breezes efface the memory of bare, leafless trees and chilling blasts which we have known at this season. In this land "where everlasting spring abides, and never-fading flowers," we wonder if indeed it can be November anywhere.

CHAPTER VIII

SANTA BARBARA

FROM earliest childhood the praises of Santa Barbara, more than of any other spot in California have been chanted in our ears; it has been pictured as the most favored haunt of Flora and Pomona, the chosen resort of poet and artist who find in its golden, *dolce far niente* atmosphere that inspiration sought in vain in harsher climes. It has offered health to the invalid, peace to the restless and broken in spirit, wealth to the investor, a perpetual delight to the visiting traveller, such as no other locality can, because forsooth, there is but one Santa Barbara in the world. Extravagant anticipations are rarely realized. Perhaps we had expected too much, or it was unfortunate that we did not visit this spot prior to our acquaintance with Pasadena, the contrast to that city's immaculate neatness and lavish cultivation being here so marked.

Yet charms Santa Barbara undoubtedly possesses of a very high order. Its climate is perhaps without a parallel. Unlike many other southern resorts which omit winter from their calendar, it omits summer also, so that there is almost no change of seasons. Its placid resident does not spend six months of every year in preparing for the remaining semester, as in less favored New England. He knows neither torrid days nor frigid nights; the wear and tear of life is reduced to a minimum, likewise it would seem its zest and highest achievement. Mercury seldom ranges higher than our average summer days, and never drops to the freezing point. The most tender flowers bloom perpetually, unless forced to rest by being deprived of irrigation. Fruits of all kinds are always ripe. Strawberry short-cake was served in the waning days of November, also green peas, and tomatoes from a plant seven years old, that had borne continually. Oh yes, a climate that can lead the world we cheerfully concede to Santa Barbara.

It is also "beautiful for situation," covering the pleasant slope from the base of the Santa Ynez mountains, which form its picturesque background, down to the lovely Bay, not unlike the Bay of Naples in contour, whose misty horizon line is broken twenty miles away by three verdant islands, one of them being used as a ranch by the largest sheep owners in the world. There is also here a pretty curving beach, too rocky however for comfortable bathing, with a swiftly-running surf that one can stand to his heart's content to enjoy, but there is no opportunity to sit and list to the wild wave's roar, for a brief moment. No hotel is erected within sight or sound of the beach, no platform, no toboggan-slide, not even a pop-corn stand. One can stand, or wade in the deep sand, and then walk away at his leisure. Here again we heartily wish that some wiser heads than our own would inform us why the air of this coast refuses to hold any saline particles in solution. In approaching the Atlantic shores one inhales its briny breath, while still some miles inland. Here, with a mighty ocean at our very gates, there is no suggestion of even moisture in the atmosphere, and yet its breezes must temper the torrid heats we should otherwise expect in this latitude.

Santa Barbara is a city of one street, leading straight as an arrow from the terminus of its long ocean pier (where steamers pause daily en route to San Diego or San Francisco), for two miles out toward the mesas, or foot hills. This unshaded thoroughfare has a fine smooth asphaltum floor, making a pleasant cleanly, though noisy driveway, whose borders are devoted almost wholly to business. Leading from this main street are short side avenues where pretty residences abound, though far less attention is paid here to the adornment of grounds than in the Eden to which our eyes have been recently accustomed. The Arlington sits pleasantly in its park of palms and flowers, and at one private residence we saw ten varieties of the passion-flower; at another twenty-two kinds of palm trees. Everything is possible in the way of floral culture, but the resident seems tired. This place, like every other in southern California, has had its boom, and energy is at low ebb under the collapse of Fortune's bubble.

Of the 8000 inhabitants which Santa Barbara boasts, the foreign element in its population is, at present, very large, about a dozen swarthy Mexican faces being met to that of every white man. This brings a rough, rowdy, surly atmosphere to the promenade most unwelcome, indeed quite unbearable to the spiritually sensitive. In fact, here as elsewhere the lady pedestrian is the observed of all observers. Woman usually drives, (a span at that), and like Jehu driveth furiously, or she rides. Equestrian exercise, for both sexes, is begun we should judge at the tender age of three years, and thereafter steadily followed at a breakneck pace. One gentleman here owns a saddle upon which by his order $4000 of Mexican coins has been affixed. Single equipages are the exception in California. Horses must be more plenty here than in Mass., for grocers, butchers, milkmen, even the John Chinamen, in collecting for their laundries, almost invariably drive a span.

The old Mission Church of Santa Barbara is

the best preserved and finest of its kind in the country. It is still occupied by holy *padres* who hold services regularly. Founded as it was, Dec. 4, 1786, which happened to be the feast-day of the somewhat obscure saint Barbara (a daughter of Dioscurus, in ancient Bithynia, beheaded by her father because of her persistent allegiance to the Christian faith), her name was given to this Mission and to the Presidio, the first old town, or fortress, which was 1000 feet square, enclosed by a high adobe wall. The walls of the church are eight feet in thickness, and we heard rumors of a garden in the rear of the sanctuary to which the appreciative eye and contaminating presence of woman is never admitted. There is also a cemetery, originally intended for the burial of Indian converts. The Indian population was once very large in this region, and no locality is richer in Indian relics. To this day the place is very slightly tinctured with the flavor of Uncle Sam's dominions, for when we offered to a fruit dealer an ordinary one dollar greenback, it was greeted with shouts of merriment, a thorough examination on all sides of the paper legal tender, with an amused estimate of how long a time had elapsed since the recipient had seen "one of them things afore."

The surrounding views are very fine, and to enjoy one of the loveliest panoramas this mundane sphere can offer, we drove to the hot springs seven miles away, situated in a wild precipitous gôrge of the Santa Ynez range, where twenty-eight springs gush forth from the face of perpendicular sandstone cliffs, at a temperature of from 120 to 130 Fahrenheit, no two fonts in this strange laboratory of Nature being impregnated alike, some so strong of sulphur as to be yellow in tint, while others are of pure arsenic. Leaving our carriages here, we walk thence a mile or more to the summit of Lookout, or Lone Mountain, by a narrow trail whose tangled undergrowth is the southern-wood, or the "old man" of our country gardens.

We reach the peak suddenly at last with a surprise that no exclamation can exhaust. Before us the glassy bay, beyond the illimitable depths of the broad, calm Pacific, at our feet and on either side the loveliest of valleys. Santa Barbara on the right is a delight to the eye, while on our left stretch the fertile fields of Carpinteria, and of Montecito, where we have viewed the largest grape vine in the world (measurements become tiresome), of Summerland, where the Spiritualists of this coast have founded a colony, on to Buenaventura, where was established a still earlier Mission, while behind and around us and them rise a succession of jagged peaks, that make of our own hardly-won height, a pigmy in comparison. We look down into fruit orchards, into acres of pampas-grass whose snowy plumes are here cultivated for the market, we trace the shining rails of what seems from this altitude a toy railway in its course along the beach for thirty miles ere it is lost between mountain walls in its five hour's search for Los Angeles. And along its narrow path, at frequent intervals, and often in most forbidding environments, are scattered sparse clusters of hamlets, whose occupants we fancy must often voice the song of Arné:

> " What shall I see if I ever go
> Over yon mountains high?"

CHAPTER IX

RIVERSIDE

PASADENA has a twin, and her name is Riverside. They are both "in verdure clad" right royally, and possess many attributes in common, resembling each other more closely perhaps in age, in rapid growth, and many minor characteristics than any other two cities of California. Pasadena is much the larger place; and while conceding to it a superior situation, a beauty of adornment, and a home-like charm found nowhere else, we must grant to Riverside the palm of fruit-culture. The acme of orange-fruitage is certainly attained here, both in extent and in quality. The orchards are indeed "groves," the trees being so large and full as to completely overshadow and hide the residences, which we know exist somewhere in their green depths.

Riverside is situated in San Bernardino County, seven miles from Colton. This county, by the way, is the largest in the United States. Within its borders fifteen States the size of "little Rhody" could be placed without crowding. The Santa

Ana river runs through the neighborhood, hence the name — Riverside — chosen for the settlement in 1871, when the gigantic scheme for irrigation was begun. The soil of Riverside is a red clay mixed with sand — washed probably from the mountain, — a most unpromising, sterile-looking soil, but needing evidently only a little scratching and a plentiful supply of water to prove itself especially adapted to fruits of all kinds. Energetic labor was not lacking in the early settlers of this happily chosen locality, and their canal system of irrigation challenges the admiration of every visitor. The river above the town was tapped, and two cemented canals constructed, twelve and fourteen miles long, ten to twenty feet wide, from which sub-canals (100 miles of them) surround every block, with gateways through which the water can be admitted to the grounds from the main artery, at pleasure.

Water is never allowed at the immediate base of an orange tree. Furrows are ploughed five or six feet from the trunk of each tree, and two or three feet apart, making perhaps three furrows between each row of trees, these furrows all connecting with each other throughout the grove, for miles in length, so that when the water is admitted from the outer surrounding channel, as it is once in thirty days during the summer, it flows gently round in little rills, where it can be best appropriated by the young rootlets. The system is perfect, and the results correspondingly rich. Over 900 car-loads of golden fruit were shipped from Riverside last year, and it is expected the crop will reach 1,200 car-loads this season.

Lemons, olives, apricots, and pomegranates are also extensively grown, and raisin culture is an important feature of Riverside industry, a quarter of a million dollars accruing last year from this product alone, which is of a quality to compete most favorably with foreign importations. The White Muscat grape is cultivated for this purpose, and if the printer renders the word Mascot, the mistake would not be a bad one, for such it has proved to many a lucky owner. The vines are planted about three feet apart, giving 660 vines to the acre, they are trimmed back to the dry stump each fall, and require comparatively little care. After the grapes are picked they are spread, while still in the field, in so-called sweat-boxes, though they do not really sweat. The moisture of the grape permeates the mass, softening the stems, and after two or three days they are sorted into three different grades of excellence, dried, winnowed, and packed ; and most interesting is it to watch one or two hundred girls, with deft fingers arranging the layers in boxes ready for shipment.

Riverside is some seven miles long and two or

three miles wide. It abounds in enticing walks and shady drives, the perennially green pepper trees drooping in graceful arches everywhere. Each block contains two and a half acres, near the centre of which the resident rears his home, and sitting there on his pleasant veranda allows the sun to do his work for him, or waits for its golden beams to be absorbed by the numberless trees around him, until they hang with golden balls and his good fortune is assured. Less attention is given here to floral embellishment than at Pasadena, although pretty gardens are very numerous, and masses of verbenas often border the curbstones. We notice another peculiarity of this California atmosphere. It not only fails to retain the briny odor of the sea, but does not readily transmit the fragrance of flowers. A certain gauge of humidity, or density of the air seems necessary to encourage this subtle floral charm. How intoxicating in our New England gardens is the sweet breath of even one heliotrope, or one stalk of tuberose! Here one has to approach the lusty growth and mammoth petals closely to invite their familiar fragrance. Tuberoses grow on and on, at their own sweet will; as soon as the flowers of one bulb have passed, another stalk springs up to take its place.

The show-card of Riverside is of course Magnolia Avenue, the finest drive it is claimed in the world. To reach it, however, a drive of three miles from our pleasant quarters at the Glenwood is necessary. Back of Riverside as at Pasadena is an arroyo, or valley, 40 feet deep and a quarter of a mile wide. Crossing this, we reach a portion of the town known as Brockton square, because its residents are all natives of that thriving city of Mass. Next comes a strip of Government land, a mile wide, and then the tract named by some New York investors, Arlington, through which the beautiful avenue runs. Its width of 132 feet is divided into a double drive by a magnificent continuous row of pepper-trees through its centre. On either side, and between the drives and the 20 feet wide promenades, is a varied growth of trees and palms, evergreens, the eucalyptus, which unless trimmed grows 8 to 15 feet in height every year, the beautiful gravilia, and at the four corners of each intersecting avenue, a magnolia tree. Extend this vista, flecked with its enchanting lights and shades, its sunbeams crossed by waving branches, for ten miles. Imagine on its outer borders a thick green hedge which encloses residences that here find frontage, or orange groves that are simply endless in every direction, their glossy green boughs weighed down with their wealth of ripened fruit, and one can readily believe it all seems too lovely to be true, like an illusion of some magician's wand.

Yet a few miles away, overlooking this valley, rise the San Bernardino mountains which mark the boundary line between fertility and sterility. Janus-like they stand, looking down on one side upon all this verdure and wonderful productiveness, on the other side upon 23,000 square miles of desert waste stretching eastward and northward in alkaline plains, sulphur deposits, and arid barren sands.

"Lo, these are parts of His ways; but the thunder of His power, who can understand? He setteth an end to darkness, and searcheth out all perfection."

CHAPTER X

SAN DIEGO

THE bay of San Diego, which forms one of the finest natural harbors in the world, was first discovered by Don Sebastian Viscaino, Nov. 10, 1602. He surveyed its waters two days later, which date happened to be the 260th anniversary of the death of San Diego, St. James de Alcala. The great explorer therefore christened his newly-found prize with the name of this patron saint, a choice approved and adopted by the Mission established here sixty years later, the earliest of the eighteen Missions founded in California, and the only one to accept a nomenclature already provided. Built in 1769, it was destroyed by an unexpected attack from the Indians in 1775; rebuilt in 1776, its only foe thereafter was the gentler but no less relentless destroyer — Time. It lies to-day a crumbling ruin, its roof fallen in, its arches open to the sky, its bells (which were cast in Spain) removed to the old village, six miles distant, where they hang suspended from a cross-beam, in the open air.

This Old Town, as it is called, the original San Diego, four miles north of the present city, is a most interesting place to visit, as being the site of the first white settlement in California, and one of the oldest in the Republic. It bears an impress of age and decay which is quite pathetic. A modern Indian school is fostered here, there is a store or two, and a motor car-runs through its one street twice a day, creating a little ripple in the prevailing stagnation, but otherwise it is filled with ruins of old adobe huts, of roofless jagged walls slowly dropping to pieces, as the numerous gophers burrow beneath them, or the harmless lizards dart in and out of each sunny crevice. One feels a veritable Rip Van Winkle in Old Town. Some of these lowly dwellings are still occupied, their doorways screened by smilax, or a dense thatching of the California morning-glory, whose large sky-blue blossoms climb in luxuriant masses to the ridge-pole, their white centres gleaming like myriad stars.

Overlooking the village, on Presidio Hill, is the half-obliterated embankment which marks the outline of Fort Stockton, a relic of stormier days. And a still more interesting link of modern reminiscence is the long low building fronting on the *plaza* designated by Mrs. Helen Hunt Jackson as the one in which Ramona was married. It was in Old Town that the gifted authoress heard the sad story of the maiden whose life she utilized for her romance, though it was a lady of Temecula whose first name suggested its title. We entered the deserted structure, and passed through its wide hall to the courtyard upon which its every room opens, the doors standing ajar, as if the rightful occupants would soon return. The exterior of the building was originally plastered but patches of the white plaster dropping away, exposes to view the brown adobe mud of its foundation walls. The roof is of the Spanish tiling which somewhat resembles large broken flower-pots, the convex and concave layers facing each other in even rows. One feels a sad pity for the homeless bride, who had fled so far from that Camulos ranch, lying away to the north of Los Angeles, and who knew not what further trials awaited her in the future, but happily love makes every burden light.

The modern city of San Diego is regularly laid out with broad avenues, suitably numbered and lettered, and very level, excepting on its northern boundary where Florence Hill rises somewhat abruptly, crowned with fine residences. Its stores have an Eastern look, and the prices of goods are very reasonable. Its people are pleasant and affable, and many are of New England birth. The chief natural charm of San Diego is undoubtably its equable climate, its uniform spring-like temperature, in summer or in winter; added to this, there is a buoyancy, a remarkable uplifting quality in the atmosphere. One does not feel that he weighs an ounce in San Diego, although the scales show a steady upward-going tendency. There are sea-turns and breezes occasionally, but these are tempered by the peninsula which lies between the Bay and the Ocean — fair Coronado.

And one attempts the description of this exceptionable seaside-resort most reluctantly, for it must be seen and felt to be thoroughly appreciated. With a temperature that allows fruits of tropical and temperate zones to ripen side by side, with a bay and an ocean on either hand, its beach one of the finest in the world, its surf magnificent, and with a radiant sunlit atmosphere that no pen can ever portray, or brush transmit, what wonder that this location was chosen for that Aladdin's palace — the Hotel del Coronado, the largest on the globe. It is a unique structure, with an architectural style of its own, stretching itself easily and gracefully over seven acres of ground, enclosing thus a courtyard where rare flowers bloom beneath the dashing spray of fountains, and palms shade the walks that lead thither from the drawing and music rooms, from rotunda and many private dining-rooms that border this garden. When at evening electric lights shed their glamour o'er the scene, touching the verdure with such livid brilliancy, when choice music adds its charm to the soft air, when fair forms picturesquely clad, float in and out from light to shadow, we realize that childhood's dreams of fairy-land were all true and are now realized. Rumors reached our celibate ears of wonderful bridal suites in unvisited regions of this vast place that are dreams of Oriental splendor, but we gained or coveted no nearer acquaintance with their white and golden elegance. Besides this hotel, a thriving little town has sprung up on the peninsula in the last three years, with an ostrich farm, and pleasant little parks. Communication with the main land is by ferry-boat.

Many delightful trips can be enjoyed from San Diego, one to Lakeside, a mountainous district in the Cajone canon, another to Ensenada, Mexico, by steamer, or, the Mexican border can also be reached by a twenty-mile ride in an open motor-car along the Bay to National City (a stirring place which still shows many evidences of a mushroom growth), through its suburbs, where olives are extensively cultivated, and from which diverges the road to Sweetwater Dam, the city's reservoir, thence across a desolate country given over to cacti of various kinds and grease-wood bushes, whose oily roots are sought for fuel, to Tia Juana where one can visit the Government building and be officially stamped, or drive to the monument marking the boundary line between California and Mexico. Smoking seems a necessary assistance to respiration with the average Mexican, and driving or lounging, his chief occupation. We saw no drivers however who irreverently tried to show Almighty God how to make a horse, for both manes and tails remained in the pristine beauty and usefulness for which their Creator designed them. The swarthy citizen returns our morning salutation with a Frenchy "*ne comprends pas*" gesture and the one word " Mexicano," albeit with gleaming teeth and the grace of a courtier. But Nature has a language which is universal. As Harry French in the Himalaya mountains heard with delight a rooster crow in unmistakable English, so we can testify that the wind sighs through the harp-strings of a stunted Mexican pine, with a real New Hampshire twang.

But one of the most charming spots to visit in the vicinity of San Diego, and one which the public has heard far too little about is La Jolla (pronounced *La Holya*, and signifying The Hole), on the Pacific coast north of the city. The route thither lies through Old Town, where we view again the mouldering embers of a life above whose grave no *resurgam* will ever be written, we see the two lofty date palms planted by the *padres* over 100 years ago, their 370 olive trees of the same age being also in good bearing condition, and, turning westward reach the coast at Pacific

Beach, four miles from La Jolla, whence a meandering carriage road leads to this natural curiosity.

The precipitous clay cliffs at this point are not only serpentine in outline, affording shelter to numerous bays and inlets, but they are cut by the action of the waves into caves, grottos and arches in which the surf holds high carnival, though at low tide the visitor can pass under fantastic natural bridges into these weird rocky caverns. Far grander however is it to sit on some high ledge above the tumult when the breakers are at their height, and watch them assail our fortress with deafening roar. Sometimes two rollers from opposite directions will strive to enter at once the cave beneath us, reverberating through the rocky chambers with an explosion like artillery, then after a moment's space, the spray and foam are thrown back into the outer air and high above our heads, transfixed there for a brief instant by a beautiful rainbow's arch, as if the sea-nymph whose home the rude waves had so roughly invaded, resentful of such intrusion, had tossed back a handful of her jewels after the retreating foe.

Indeed, color is everywhere dominant at La Jolla. Bright red and crimson mosses are washed up on the sand; the shells, even the minutest, are of brilliant tints, the water while very clear is in places a mosaic of blue and nile-green patches, while gold-fishes of lusty size turn up their gleaming scales to catch and reflect the sunshine. The sky is of the bluest and tenderest tone. The rarified air is so invigorating, so fresh and fragrant that we deliberately tasted of one opaline wave to make sure that we were looking upon an ocean of brine. One trophy from La Jolla which we especially prize is a shark's egg that had been washed up on the rocks, black as india-rubber and spirally convoluted like a shell. Spouting whales are frequently observed from one promontory of this beach.

Returning from a day spent at this delightful spot, we reach San Diego just as the sun is sinking behind Point Loma, whose white lighthouse is clearly outlined against the crimson background, a brilliancy which touches the myriad windows of the Coronado with flame, and is reflected in the placid waters of the bay, when, suspended above the horizon, in mirage, (a phenomenon common to this luminous locality), appears a three-masted ship with every sail set, being towed by an energetic tug into some shoreless harbor of the upper air.

CHAPTER XI

EN ROUTE

AFTER every enjoyable trip through southern California, one naturally returns again and again to peerless Pasadena, which like a sweet-voiced siren woos and attracts us, potently and irresistibly. Certainly no enchantress owns more willing captives, for Pasadena seems lovelier than ever since the recent showers have clothed her hills and lawns with richest verdure, and fringed her orange boughs with tassels of lightest emerald green. The old walks and drives offer fresh delights, while new ones still invite us. We visit the garden of Mrs. Dr. Carr, a lady well known as a botanist, who has collected in her extensive grounds a specimen of almost every tree, shrub, or flower known to temperate or tropical climes. On her lawn stands a large camphor tree, a cedar of Lebanon, (worthy to have been chosen by Solomon's builders), an Oregon cedar from the Columbia river valley, a red-wood, a variety of pines, palms, bananas with ripening bunches of fruit and curious blossoms suspended therefrom, while in another corner are persimmon trees whose branches are breaking under their weight of luscious fruitage. The view from these grounds also of the city, the valley, and cloud-wreathed mountain range is exceedingly beautiful.

Pasadena has also, at present, an added attraction. The Raymond is open and its first winter occupants have arrived. The eminence on which the hotel so grandly stands, and the sloping sides of this charming height have received the last touch of adornment which cultivated taste and ingenuity could devise. Masses of color form effective contrasts everywhere, while beyond the garden beds, springing up from the lawn, are oleanders, double daturas and, azaleas willing to blossom out of doors as well as under glass roofs, interspersed with slender evergreens which cast dark slanting shadows over the *alfalfa* which forms much of the green sward in this latitude. 'And at evening, when darkness veils all this loveliness, the hillside presents a new phase of beauty which can be seen for miles around. Electric lights line every path and drive, winding about from base to summit like wandering fireflies, which with the lighted windows of the hotel remind us of that piece of pyrotechnic display frequently given on Boston Common, Fourth of July nights, called the illuminated Beehive, from which swarming bees dart out into the air and return on fiery wing.

But the warm afternoon's glow flooded the hill when we ascended to the open portals of this famous house, pausing as we went to admire the magnificent roses, the heliotrope trees so lavish of their purple bloom as to veil therewith their leaves, stopping often to wonder over some strange plant or new flower, turning even when the broad veranda is reached to gaze with glistening eyes upon the rare beauty of the more distant landscape, until half-reluctantly we seek the hitherto coveted pleasure of entering this charming place. And of course when once within the spacious portals the first thing we behold is the genial presence of Mr. Merrill, with "Crawford's" so plainly written all over his rotund personality. How natural he looks! And so strong is the power of association that instantly that part of us which is not anchored is whisked away to that grand old Notch among the White Hills, around which cluster so many pleasant memories. How desolate it must be to-day, swept by chilling blasts, with deep snows drifting about the closed doors and shutters and pleasant paths. Do those lovely cascades leap and splash and lash themselves into foam when no human eye beholds, no heart responds to their wild beauty? Do those mountain brooks ripple and purl and chatter in never-ending play, or has the Frost-king laid his icy fingers upon their breasts and stilled their merry frolic?

But the strains of other music, the fragrance of calla lilies grouped in vases near, recall us to a sunnier land as we are led from the rotunda into the reception room, thence through the ladies' billiard parlor and reading room into the long drawing room where the usual orchestral concert, given each afternoon and evening, is in progress. The musicians are grouped about the grand piano, about which rests a large pyramid of chrysanthemums; ladies sit around the room with their embroideries and fancy work, gentlemen drop their newspapers to toy with their glasses and listen to the choice programme, while the warm June (we mean December) sunshine casts long slanting beams through this beautiful room. Across the corridor is the spacious ball-room, with its little stage and proscenium arch for the dramatically inclined. This room is frescoed with very bold design in natural tints of brake ferns, palms, and cannas, which lend a most effective adornment to the place. Natural flowers fill every table, nook and vase, in tasteful combinations. They are placed as an appetizing feature upon every table in the dining-room, where the silver and dainty napery form a most effective background for floral display, as indeed they prove for the strawberries and cream served in mid-winter at the Raymond with the matutinal meal.

If winter were one long playtime hour, how

pleasant, how restful to loiter here, but other scenes invite us, new duties await us on the Northern coast. Therefore most regretfully we break one by one the meshes of the enchantress' net, and speed our way onward, beholding with our last yearning glance on one side the train, the new white mantle which the night has spread upon the loftiest peaks of the Sierra, while flashing past our window on the other hand is golden fruit growing ever larger and of brighter hue, with a goodly crop of windfalls bestrewing the ground beneath. How long would they thus remain, if the street gamins we have known should invade this land?

The route from Los Angeles to San Francisco runs through a sparsely settled, unpopulous but very picturesque region. The character of the scenery may be inferred from the fact that the railway pierces some thirty tunnels, so grudgingly do the mountain spurs relinquish the right of way. The passage through the longest of these tunnels, at San Fernando, requires nearly as much time as does our own Hoosac, though not quite two miles long, as for some reason, (perhaps from the shelving character of the rock hereabouts), the utmost care and the slowest pace of our iron steed is enforced. In direct contrast to these rocky walls which hem us in so closely, we next traverse the western corner of the great Mojave desert, a level sandy plain, not wholly devoid of vegetation, for here the yucca palm abounds, utilized we hear by a London firm for the manufacture of printing paper. Then as the darkness settles we enter a spur of the Sierra Nevada range and the scenery becomes grand and awe-inspiring. It is a singular fact that time-tables are made up in this country with especial design, it would seem, to pass by the most interesting feature of every journey after nightfall, when there is no good reason why the train should not start out earlier. Consequently the grandeur of Tehachapi summit was gained by our two panting locomotives just as every berth was made up and their owners were expected to occupy them. Perish the thought! We had heard of that triumph of railway engineering known as the Loop, and were determined at any cost to see it or — die! So, impressing a railway official and his big lantern with an all-consuming desire to inspect this part of the country just once more himself, we, under his escort traversed six open and very breezy platforms, and five cars filled with the oddest shaped sleeping human bundles, to the rear end of the long train where we hung on to the brake-wheel (realizing as never before what a non-conductor of heat iron is) and thence for several miles, we were lost to all but the sublimity of this wild mountain pass.

We could look up, up until the stars seemed

lower than the topmost trees, we looked down into chasms and ravines that made our narrow ledge upon the mountain's breast seem a most precarious footing. How deep and solemn the shadows beneath us, how soft and silvery the young moon's light upon the crests, illuminating also our narrow course, while a lesser luminary, the kind lantern, answered more questions than it had ever thought of before. Doubtless it will avoid a Yankee in future as it would a cyclone.

But the Loop? Well, it was longer than we expected, being some three or four miles in circumference, therefore the curve was very gradual. The loop is necessary because the grade of two adjacent defiles is of such different elevation, that the only way to pass from one to the other is by this little detour, the train in returning crossing its own track by a tunnel underneath the road-bed just passed over.

From this point onward we found one of the roughest bits of railway travel we ever experienced. We had to keep awake and *hold on* to remain in our berths. Precipitation into the aisle seemed momentarily imminent. Perhaps we missed the vestibule cars to which we have of late been accustomed, which reduces the friction of travel to a minimum. But we were not left without other Raymond provision for our comfort, even though travelling alone. Long ago in that Boston office, these managers knew that we should need on this journey both supper and breakfast, consequently a coupon entitling us to each repast was found bound into our russia-leather, gilt-edged ticket-books.

Soon after daybreak, as we leave Lathrop, (this town bearing the maiden name of the wife of ex-Gov. and Senator Leland Stanford), we cross the San Joaquin river, the first river we have seen in California that has not been bottom side up, the sandy river-bed alone visible. The land is level as a prairie and beautifully verdant. Woods are occasionally seen which give a home feature to the landscape, although the growth is chiefly live-oak and eucalyptus. Green hills arise on the horizon as we near our destination, double-peaked Mount Diablo claims our admiration, a portion of San Francisco bay is skirted, and soon we alight, not in the metropolis as we had a right to expect, but in Oakland, whence we embark in a commodious ferry-boat and finish our journey by water. Could anything be more incongruous? To approach San Francisco from Boston by ploughing the blue waters of the bay and landing at the city's water-front, exactly as if we came from Japan! Is this not sailing under false pretences? In vain we are told that San Francisco is a peninsula, that the bay runs around it so completely that approach to it by land is impossible. We are still unreconciled. Isn't Boston a peninsula? And would not a visitor from Chicago feel outraged if he were obliged to reach the Hub by way of Hull?

CHAPTER XII

SAN FRANCISCO

SO magnificent a harbor as San Francisco Bay, one in which the combined navies of the world might easily find commodious anchorage, demanded as a natural sequence that a populous and cosmopolitan city should be built upon its shores. The fact that the site chosen for the city was a succession of hills and ridges proved no insurmountable obstacle. We had heard that San Francisco was built upon one hundred hills. We have not counted them, but do not believe the number overestimated. And *such* hills! The usual comparison "steep as the roof of a house" does only partial justice to their acute incline. Nothing could climb some of them it would seem but a cat or a squirrel, and yet up their successive and thickly settled terraces mount steadily and speedily the cable cars with which the city is completely honeycombed in every direction, naught but the tops of their roofs being visible to the observer at the foot of the hill. And, reaching the summit, the cars pitch almost perpendicularly downward as a fly descends the walls of a room, or as a ship dips into the trough of a heavy sea, only to mount a higher and steeper hill beyond, continuing this see-sawing,

"Now we go up, up, up-y;
And now we go down, down, down-y,"

style of locomotion for miles all over the city. Exaggeration here is an impossibility, for it is all so utterly incredible, even while we gaze. To quote from a Santa Barbara stage driver: "What's the use of lying about this country, when the truth is more than any one can believe?"

And on these precipitous heights and the approaches leading thereto stand magnificent palaces, residences of the *elite*, the supplies for which, as well as their building materials must have been obtained, we naturally infer, by air-line from some other planet, since the streets on these upper terraces are grass-grown from curb to curb, except where it is cut by the cable track. These homes of wealth and refinement surround themselves often with beautiful grounds and gardens which flourish marvellously in this etherealized air, while from these summits the views of the bay and ocean and of the great city which stretches like a vast amphitheatre below us, are surpassingly grand.

Many of these hills have been leveled to fill up as many valleys, swamps and ravines, (so masterfully does the mind of man triumph over all obstacles), and the business portion of the city is therefore broad and level, with plenty of room in its marts of trade, in its wide avenues and on its pavements for everybody, at the busiest hour. We have seen no blockades, no crowding, no pushing or jostling, and, although *this* statement will hardly be credited in suburban Boston, no cars in which human beings are packed like cattle in the shambles. One can ride without being trodden under foot, or being sat upon, without carrying the weight of one neighbor's bundles upon his knee, or the print of another's elbow in his side for an hour or two after reaching his destination. And yet what a noisy, tumultuous, wide-awake city it is, for it never sleeps. It is always up and dressed. If we arise at the "wee sma' hours ayant the twal'," and look from our casement into the street below, we see stores open, houses brilliantly lighted, cable-cars with clanging alarm-bell whizzing by, merry strollers whistling under our window, strains of distant music in the air, and the same features of activity that belong to daylight. Observance of the Sabbath is quite an obsolete custom, perhaps because of the foreign mixture in the population.

The richness of the city and the lavish display of its wealth cannot fail to impress the visitor. Such wonderful shop-windows, the like of which Boston, even at her holiday season, never dreamed, for San Francisco seems the nautilus to secrete the pearls of the sea, to gather to herself the choicest treasures of every market and every land. Even thus have brave souls and noble characters from many nations contributed to her greatness, whose names she appropriately immortalizes in the nomenclature of her streets. One familiar with the early history of her pioneer days feels the blood quicken in his veins as he reads the names of Fremont and Taylor, of the army, Montgomery, Stockton and Dupont, of the navy, Sutter, Howard, Leavenworth, Jones, Vallejo, Larkin and Geary, the first postmaster, and first agent authorized by the P. O. Dept. to bring mail to the Pacific coast, later chosen alcalde, an office similar to that of mayor. It was in a churchyard on Geary street that the sacred dust was laid, so dear to many Boston hearts, the form once vitalized and enshrined by the matchless spirit of Thomas Starr King. The city ordinance forbidding burials in the city's precincts was set aside in this instance that the sight of his tomb might recall as a daily inspiration his valued words and work. But as the old church has now withdrawn to a more quiet locality, the treasured ashes have been also tenderly removed to another resting place, which is still however within the city limits.

And of Chinatown — that ulcer gnawing at the city's heart — this deponent speaketh not. It occupies a large tract of one of the best portions of the city. We have passed through its most civilized and cleanliest corner, where are the shops filled with strange and often valuable curios, much sought after by Eastern visitors. But of the opium dens, two and three stories below the level of the street, leading from alleys two feet wide only to be threaded under the protection of the police, of the theatres whose performances sometimes last twelve hours, and of other abodes of filth and vermin, the profoundest ignorance would seem the greater bliss. If one has a retentive memory let him be careful what pictures he hangs among her cherished treasures, selecting only those whose permanent companionship will be a pleasure. As well eat tainted meat as contact from motives of curiosity alone, impure malarial mental atmospheres.

The trip to the Cliff House and its attendant attractions is a deservedly popular one. The hotel occupies a rocky promontory on the coast outside the Golden Gate, upon which and the Fort that guards this open portal we look down as we wind our tortuous course about the bluffs. The heights above the Cliff House are occupied by the private grounds of Mr. Adolph Sutro, and are thrown freely open for the public to enjoy. A distinguishing feature of this extensive garden and park is the abundance of statuary with which it is peopled, both classic and comic. Opposite the hotel, a stone's throw from the precipitous face of the cliff are the small rocky islands upon which a squirming, writhing mass of seal-skin cloaks in the rough lay drying in the sun. This is the natural habitat of these semi-aquatic creatures and a law has been passed, forever preserving them from injury. Least lovely of Nature's large family, and certainly most uncomfortable, their hideous wailing and barking are the bane of the place, for this caterwauling never ceases day or night, but greatly increases in stormy weather. The beach below the cliff is very gradual in its slope towards the water which makes a magnificent surf and rapid breakers.

Returning to the city, a visit can be paid *en route* to Golden Gate Park, an enclosure of over a thousand acres, which only a few years ago was an utterly barren sand bank, but has now been magically transformed into a paradise. Its trees are so thickly planted that at times one seems in an impenetrable forest, the winding drives and paths lead the eye such a short distance before reaching the vanishing point. The landscape gardening, the ornamental beds in quaint designs have also this advantage, that they are made for the whole year and not for a brief summer's day. The extensive conservatories (for which the valuable collection of the late James Lick furnished the nucleus) are filled with the choicest botanical treasures of the entire world. Floating on one of its miniature lakes, beside our white pond-lily in lavish bloom, we noted the mammoth leaves of the Victoria Regia, or Amazon water-lily. Statues to Garfield and Halleck stand in the Park, also a handsome memorial to Francis Scott Key, the author of our "Star Spangled Banner."

The Presidio, a military reservation of 1500 acres, occupies a lovely spot on the northern outskirts of San Francisco, just within the Golden Gate, and on the margin of the bay. The fortified island of Alcatraz is here a near neighbor, and some invalid members of its garrison were spending, on the occasion of our visit, a comfortable convalescence in the Presidio hospital. The officers' homes were exceedingly pleasant, being surrounded by lawns and gardens, and a little park whose serpentine paths were outlined with cannon balls. The quarters assigned to the horses of the cavalry and artillery were most comfortable, and the private soldier and guardian of our peace seemed to have no duty on hand more arduous than a game of base-ball.

The Spanish *padres* who, in California's early days so industriously and zealously planted their Missions at every point whose occupancy seemed of importance in the success of their purpose to christianize the land and to awe the native tribes into submission, showed most excellent judgment in the selection of sites. The mission edifices were always situated where the land was most fertile and always removed some distance from the coast, although such selection must often have added many weary miles to the lonely journeys of the fathers in their visits to widely separated diocese.

The Mission Dolores of San Francisco however (built in 1776), was not so far removed from the bay as it now seems, since so much land has been reclaimed from the sea by man's device and necessity, in fact, in a recent excavation for a cellar on Montgomery street, quite in the business heart of the city, the hulk of a sloop was found which had originally sunk at its moorings at the dock. A visit to the old Spanish quarter, with its relics of early settlement, offers vivid contrast to the lofty edifices of more modern sections. The sanctuary itself is the smallest we have seen of its kind and very quaint in its exterior. It is of considerable length though low in height, and its façade, of greyish plaster is very narrow with two short pillars on either side, and in niches in the pediment above the entrance are hung three small bells. Its roof is of the semi-cylindrical tiling, the floor of earth and the whole structure presents a very singular and foreign appearance. Adjoining it is an ancient burial ground where some of the earlier settlers were entombed, but its present appearance is one of dilapidation and neglect. On the other side of the old Mission rises the Catholic church now used, a brick edifice with cheery interior, its walls hung with pictured object-lessons, necessary perhaps for the untutored mind before it has grown to apprehend spiritual truth, a needed step in the spiral stairway sloping God-ward.

Back of this old settlement rise the mission peaks from whose heights a new idea of the city's vast extent can be obtained. Near at hand a few adobe walls still stand; from thence the human tide swells on and stretches far and wide until its highest crest is reached on Nob Hill, where rise the palaces of the Floods, the Crockers, Stanfords and others to whom life has proved a financial success. One can almost see how the city grew and crystallized into its present form, which is still but a prophecy of its future greatness.

As an easy stepping stone from the Spanish *regime* to the days of the Argonauts, the forty-niners, one naturally turns aside to visit the beautiful building erected by the Society of Pioneers, and its relic-hall, where are collected not alone Indian and natural curiosities peculiar to California, but trophies from the entire world. Occupying a prominent place is the portrait of John W. Marshall, who on Jan. 19, 1848, first discovered gold in California, at Sutter's Mill,

Colonna, near Sacramento, and, preserved in a glass case is a fac simile of the valuable nugget which he found. On the wall hangs also a still more interesting relic — the Bear Flag — which marks the first attempt to Americanize California, or to wrest it from Mexican control and make of it an independent Republic. The flag was first raised June 14, 1846, was kept flying with great effort for twenty-seven days, and lowered July 11th, to be gladly replaced by the stars and stripes as then authorized by the U. S. government, between whom and Mexico war had been declared. The flag is of white unbleached cotton a yard long, with a four-inch border of red flannel. In the upper left-hand corner is a lone star, in the centre a grizzly bear, rampant, these designs being executed without artistic excellence, in Venetian red and Spanish brown from some wheelwright's shop, while underneath in ink are the words CALIFORNIA REPUBLIC. The name California was originally a fancy title given by the obscure Spanish author of a novelette, to the imaginary territory lying northward of Mexico, as vaguely reported by Cortes on his return to the court of Spain.

CHAPTER XIII

OAKLAND

SIX miles from San Francisco, as the sea-gull flies, across the pleasant waters of the bay, stands the beautiful city of Oakland, with Alameda and Berkeley on either side. Oakland has been called the city of residences (or in slang parlance, Frisco's bedroom), and it wears the title appropriately. It has a diurnal population of about 65,000, and while possessing a thriving little business centre of its own, its wide level streets are chiefly occupied by beautiful villas and homes. The gardens which surround them remind us at this winter season of Pasadena taking a nap, and an opossum kind of nap too, a partial rest with one eye open, for Nature never sleeps in this wondrous land. Everywhere rose bushes are bristling with buds that await only a few more days of sunshine to expand, magnolias promise even earlier unfoldment, and the callas are already in their prime; indeed Oakland seems pre-eminently their chosen home, for every yard displays its abundant share of these snowy, mammoth flowers. And we note here such variety of trees from the native live-oak, (whose abundance christened the city), the locust and cottonwood, to the ornate, feathery-leaved acacia, in its many subdivisions, the mustard, fig, cypress, and numberless varieties of palms. We counted fifteen new specimens of trees and shrubs which we had never seen before, in one short walk, and were obliged to remain in ignorance as to their proper classification, for the resident, to the manor born, never knows, and doesn't even know that he does not know. Repeatedly we have asked the rightful owner and proprietor of a garden the name of a prominent flowering shrub, and then watched his changes of expression from surprise at the query to amazement and chagrin at the discovery that he cannot give you the desired information, a frank confession of his ignorance, and resolve that he will soon ascertain, but — he never will. The Californian type of mind is not of an inquiring nature. In its font of ideas there are few interrogation points. It is so much easier to take things for granted. We recently discovered a new and beautiful tree with dark, rich, glossy foliage, springing up from the sidewalk, so we took our stand beneath it, Casabianca-like, with a Spartan resolve that, come one, come all, this tree should flee from its firm base as soon as we, until we discovered its name, and there we stood, courteously inquiring of every passer-by, the thick, the thin, the short, the tall, of childhood and old age, all of whom, with true Western cordiality, regretted to the depths of their kind hearts that they were unable to serve us in some way, but alas, they couldn't unless they could, could they? One lady confessed to having lived opposite the tree for a dozen years, she knew a tree stood there, but had "never thought," what kind of a tree it was, so, as we couldnt spend the night in the street, we at last moved on, as ignorant as before.

The social atmosphere of Oakland is genial, quiet, restful and receptive to the advanced thought of the day. For this and many other reasons the traveller is induced to cast anchor in this calm haven and taste the rare pleasure of a long sojourn in this lovely place, indeed a life-sentence could be delightfully served out, here. The climate, while not so mild in winter as southern resorts, knows no sultry weather in mid-summer. Its sky is often blue and serene when a small hurricane is blowing through the streets of the larger city across the bay. There is a beautiful lake in the eastern part of Oakland surrounded by handsome villas, and in every direction there are the most enticing walks and drives, one of especial charm leading out to Piedmont, situated as its name implies, on the foot-hills of the Contra Costa range. A more magnificent view than the one obtained from this height can hardly be imagined. Oakland lies at our feet like a crescent moon; just beyond, Alameda stretches her long arm into the blue bay; on the further shore of this broad expanse of waters, San Francisco sits on her many hills, while others still higher rise behind her. From our vantage ground we can look straight through the Golden Gate, in whose royal portals the white masts of coming and departing vessels are tipped with flame in the light of the setting sun, which makes a long lane of glory between the green islands of this inland sea. What peace rests upon it! What diverse craft here find anchorage! At present there are Her Britannic Majesty's flag-ship Swiftshire, our own Charleston, in virgin white from stem to stern, a French man-of-war, and the Chinese mail steamer, together with sloops, whalers, ferry-boats and tugs innumerable, plying busily in every direction.

And as we gaze, thought reverts to two departures which these calm waters have recently witnessed. In the early hours of a smoky morning as we sat reading in the cabin of a ferry, a sudden shriek from our whistle, followed by a succession of piercing toots brought us to our feet to see what disaster was pending, when behold, close at hand lay the Japan steamer, Oceanic, with a tug at her side receiving on board a small piece of womanhood which then sped away for the Oakland mole, where a special train awaited the arrival of Nelly Bly. A narrow strip of marsh land was all which the fair traveler beheld of this glorious neighborhood, in her race against time and the advertising interests of her enterprising employers, but then — she will return.

The other young woman, who with a different kind of bravery stepped on board the Australia at high noon, bound for the Sandwich Islands, goes to return no more. The brick walls of San Francisco as they vanished from her gaze, comprised the last large city which Sister Rose Gertrude (Miss Fowler) will probably ever see, as her self-imposed exile among the lepers is for life.

A cloud of smoke which is seldom lifted hangs above San Francisco, but tree-embowered, garden-fringed, flower-crowned Oakland invites the admiring eye to linger long and tenderly upon all her verdant beauty, her broad level streets and beautiful homes. We heartily voice the apostrophe of that strange genius, poet, and large-hearted man, Joaquin Miller, who from his almond-grove on a contiguous height looks down upon this fair city and craves no other retreat:

> "Thou Rose-land! Oak-land, thou mine own!
>   Thou Sun-land! Leaf-land! Land of seas
> Wide crescented in walls of stone!
>   Thy lion's mane is to the breeze!
> Thy tawny, sun-lit lion steeps
> Leap forward as the lion leaps!

* * *

Be this my home till some fair star,
  Stoops earthward and shall beckon me!
For surely Godland lies not far
  From these Greek heights and this great sea.
My friend, my lover, trend this way;
Not far along lies Arcady."

CHAPTER XIV

THE RAINY SEASON

WE have heard that the difference between the wet and the dry season in California is that in summer it never rains, but sometimes does, while in winter it is expected to rain, but usually does not. In Southern California we found it the prevalent custom of the elements to rain at night and clear off brightly each morning, but this particular rainy season has discounted the memory of the oldest inhabitant, and broken California's record for 30 years. We are glad to have seen it, and to know what "a hard winter" is like, in this locality. We have been amused when reference has been made here to the tough weather for it is nothing more than we are accustomed to, the year round, in New England. There, we never enjoy week after week, month succeeding month of perpetual unclouded sunshine, as it is the rule to expect in this golden land. Consequently, when a series of showers follow one another here, or two or three rainy days occur in one week, the wet weather is beyond precedent. But the rain is never frozen, there are no snow drifts to wade through with chilled toes and frost-bitten ears, no chilling blasts, no leafless trees, or seared lawns. Flowers bloom on, and green ivy runs rampant over fences, door-posts, and arches.

In higher altitudes of this broad state, where the rain has been frozen, in the mountain passes and gorges of the Sierra, where snow and ice have held potent sway, the winter that is now passing will long be remembered. For seventeen days we had no communication with the Eastern states. Water in *one* form made a barrier, which all the force of water in its most potent form could not overthrow. It was a contest between ice and steam with myriad snow-flake battalions as daily re-enforcement for the enemy. The victory was finally won by the strong sinewy muscle of brawny arms with a resolute will to direct them.

And now the winter, or the rainy season is considered past. The voice of the spring is already heard, the hills that surround San Francisco and Oakland are assuming the most delicate tints of emerald green. Daily, as we watch them, we see this living tide creep higher and higher up the slopes, and dip down into the numberless dimples and dales of the verdant range, reflecting the light at such different angles, holding also such wealth of shade that the effect is that of a huge chameleon. Wild flowers begin to appear abundantly.

Large bunches of fragrant violets are seen on the street, and the beautiful acacia trees, of which there are countless varieties, are a mass of brilliant bloom. All this is very unlike Februarys which we have known, and prevents our fullest commiseration with the natives over the hardest winter they have ever experienced. Fields of wild mustard have donned their yellow caps, showing also varieties with white and with lavender blossoms. The prevalence of yellow however, in all wild flowers is very noticeable. Symbol of light — God's first-born — it is also the color-emblem of Wisdom. Blue, which symbolizes Truth, is rarest in the floral kingdom, as indeed is its correspondence in a world so rife with error that it has not yet solved Pilate's old query: "What is truth."

The winter has afforded us in this neighborhood two new years' celebrations, one arranged and decreed by old Father Thomas and the other almanac makers, which was observed in regular Fourth of July fashion, with fish-horns and bells and parties of young people going from house to house and singing the night away under friendly windows; the other (decided by the new moon) occurred a fortnight later, in Chinatown, with a great popping of fire-crackers and explosive bombs, with decorations and an unearthly din, called by courtesy music, with much feasting and social interchange, the Chinese women for this one day in all the year throwing off the yoke of abject slavery—think of that my free-born (unmarried) sisters—and looking exactly as if they had just stepped from off a fan. Mongolian gents were seen with light pea green silk trousers belted in at the ankle, a pink tunic and blue sleeveless jacket outside of all. It is safe to assert that the passage of Time was appropriately observed.

Since that festive date, our great and glorious United States government has shown its valor and prowess by deliberately strangling the life out of one half-witted little Chinaman, too foolish to understand the nature of his crime, or the justice (?) of his sentence, his only remark on hearing the verdict being "Me go back Chinee, all samee." Following the execution, scores of little newsboys at an age which should exemplify the innocence of childhood, were employed to shout through the streets every detail of the revolting spectacle, which brutal and degrading recital sows in susceptible hearts the seeds of a harvest of crime which this country will inevitably some day reap. *No* murder, judicial or otherwise, ever encourages righteousness of thought or action.

The first excursion party to register at the Palace Hotel from Pasadena, recently arrived and report a charming winter at The Raymond, where everything is done for the amusement and entertainment of its patrons. Especially was this true of the merry Christmas tide. On Christmas eve a tree was prepared on the little stage of the large auditorium. A real live Santa Claus came down from his polar retreat, and drove his sleigh and span of real Shetland ponies into and around the brilliantly lighted ball-room, gay with its decorations and the festive toilettes of the lords and ladies there assembled. Alighting at the foot of the tree, he summoned two silver-winged fairies to his side, and through their fleet aid, distributed a beautiful gift to every guest, after which dancing and feasting were enjoyed to a late hour. Every evening during that week and the next had its well-arranged programme of games, tableaux, concerts and hops.

These newly-arrived friends gave fragrant proof that the orange and lemon groves of Pasadena are now in blossom. The buds of the lemon are quite mauve in tint, although the open flower is as snowy white as its more popular sister.

Everywhere in California at all seasons, the Eastern visitor notes with surprise the abundance of *time* which the resident has on his hands. How plainly we recall the nervous tension, pressure, and strain of that Boston atmosphere, the constant endeavor to crowd a few more duties into an already over-full day, in this easy-going land where nothing and nobody ever hurries, where even the business world does not bestir itself to break its fast until an hour which the New England housewife would pronounce "shiftless," when even the cobbler who is needed to adjust one's boot-heel cannot be found on duty till midway of the forenoon. We doubt if a dog ever caught a cat in this latitude; we certainly have never seen one try. Perhaps they are too courteous, a quality so marked in their exceedingly polite owners.

The same air of elegant leisure characterizes the management here of the postal department. King Wanamaker's business requires no haste in this country. A letter recently mailed in San Francisco to a friend three or four streets away, was delivered after an interval of two days and nights. Mail seems to be regarded with supreme indifference by the resident, who would accept the receipt of an important letter to-morrow, as complacently as to-day. In two southern cities in this State where papers and pamphlets have accumulated beyond the convenience of the carriers, they (the papers, not the carriers) have been deliberately burned in open bonfire, or dumped into the bay, a disregard for private preference, or the importance of current literature, which the transient tourist takes unkindly.

CHAPTER XV

SONOMA COUNTY

IT is less in the large cities, where specimens of every nation, clime and tongue, with all conceivable amalgamations compose their cosmopolitan element, than in the outlying districts, the fertile valleys, or old mining sections, that typal California can best be studied. The next county north of San Francisco, comprising the Russian river and other valleys, is a vast garden in its productiveness, while it abounds in grand and picturesque scenery. It is a great fruit-bearing region, and its chief industries are the canning of fruits and the manufacture of wines.

To visit this valley we take a little steamer at her dock in San Francisco and sail up the bay along the city's water front, past cannon-bristling Alcatraz, in sight of the Presidio, crossing the roadway to the Gate through which the bland wind blows fiercely and the rough waves rock our boat like a cradle, still on by the little bay village of Saucelito, a veritable Downer's Landing for picnickers and yachtsmen, though unlike the latter resort it is built up and down the steep sides of a green hill; on the other hand passing the military station on Angel island, most perfect in all its appointments even to the little white-spired church half discernible above the tree-tops, until we reach Tiburon where we take the train to continue our delightful journey by land.

The first stopping-place of note is San Rafael, the Nahant for Frisco's wealthy merchants. It is a pretty place, with its fine residences almost hidden by tall trees, and its large and handsome Hotel Rafael. From this point the ascent of Mount Tamalpais can be made, an imposing summit which rears its head 2000 feet above the bay and commands a wide-extended view of land and ocean, of cities, towns and sister mountain heights. From this point, after the eclipse of four tunnels of considerable length, we emerge into the verdant Russian river valley of Sonoma county, and skirt its graperies, now trimmed back to the stump though soon to become fields of luxuriant foliage, blossom and fruit, we pass almond orchards in fullest pink and white bloom, wild oak groves whose branches are hung with long festoons of Southern moss, hill-sides covered with a thick growth of the evergreen mazanita and madrona trees, while back of these rise the higher coast range and the Napa mountains.

At Petaluma, so many homes are surrounded

with acacia trees in flower, each illumined by the warm western sun, that the town seems a mass of woolen yellow snowballs as we speed by. Large huge mills are here, and a very rich territory surrounds the place whose products have a double egress to the world's commerce, since a narrow inlet from San Pablo bay affords sloop navigation to this point.

We do not pass through Sonoma, where a U. S. garrison was maintained until 1851, and at which place the Bear Flag was raised. On the occasion of a recent Fourth of July celebration, the original flag was taken from its glass-case in the Pioneers' hall in San Francisco, was carried to Sonoma, where attached to a piece of the old pole it was once more flung to the breeze. One imagines that the old grizzly, so crudely represented on the banner must wonder what has become of all his companions, once so common in this region, during his long Rip Van Winkle nap. The stars and stripes were first hoisted by Gen. Fremont at Monterey, July 7th 1846, from which date the commercial history of the state begins.

Santa Rosa, which holds the county seat, is the prettiest town in this vicinity. It claims a population of 10,000, and has an interesting legend connected with its christening. Soon after the founding of the Mission of San Rafael in 1847, Friar Amorosa started forth in search of natives whom he could by force of arms convert to the true faith. He met with only one stray Indian maiden, who was wandering alone near the site of the present town. This girl was seized by the zealous Father, dragged by that exponent of muscular Christianity to an adjacent creek and forcibly baptized as Santa Rosa. Her tribe aroused by the outcry, and not duly appreciating this energetic effort for her sanctification, obliged the devout proselyter to flee to the shelter of the Sonoma mission, and history is silent concerning the future career of the dusky heathen maid, save that her pretty name was given to the settlement which soon arose in this locality.

Healdsburg, the next place of importance, a sleepy little town, is situated at the fork of Russian river and Dry Creek, a tributary whose turbulent flow at this season belies its name. There is here a pretty wooded eminence, named Fitch mountain for one of the early settlers, and more imposing heights beyond skirt the horizon. The extinct volcano of Mt. St. Helena, 4,850 feet high, though situated in Napa county is a prominent landmark, and bears evidence by the ermined mantle which now drapes its shoulders that its once fiery heart is cold and still, yet lava deposits in various sections of the valley give silent witness of former activity. On its summit also can be found sea-shells and other tokens of a submarine experience which it has known, whose details no pen will ever describe.

Another height is known as Geyser Peak, at whose base are found the only geysers in California. To visit these we continue our journey northward to Cloverdale, whence a long stage-drive over a mountain road too narrow for the passage of but one vehicle, except in rare instances, (at which points we naturally share the solicitude of the old lady who wanted to turn out and wait until a team came by), conveys us to our destination. Whether this terminus can be called Paradise or Purgatory, we have not determined. Grandeur and beauty of scenery above and round about us; below a wild mountain gorge whose trail can be followed a mile or more, or as far as the soles of one's boots can endure the unwonted temperature of mother earth, whose usually placid breast throbs, and trembles, mutters, moans and puffs in tumultuous unrest. We have never seen her in this mood before. Her gnomes are in rebellion, or are holding high carnival with elfish imps from some nether world. But their frolic is less boisterous than it was some years ago, their natural ebullition having been quelled by the visiting vandals who have dropped stones in these natural craters and tunnels, and thus diverted the upheaval into other channels.

In some of these geysers, large stones and

sticks are blown aside like bits of paper. Some eject only vapor, others have a regular pulsating action like machinery, notably one known as the devil's grist-mill. There is also the witches' cauldron, and the devil's ink-stand, filled with the blackest liquid, often borne away in vials by tourists to inscribe their names therewith upon the hotel register. There are springs and basins of every color, temperature, taste, smell and chemical property. There are gentle moans and loud explosions, quiet and forceful eruptions, and every manner of expression of Nature's forceful energy.

There is also in Sonoma county a petrified forest, the trees lying in two tiers over a tract a mile in extent, the largest single tree measuring 68 feet in length by 11 feet in diameter. When found, they were covered with volcanic ashes and atoms of silica.

Large stories are told in this region of the days when agricultural interests were sacrificed to those of mining, and the prosy occupation of farming found few adherents, when gold dust became the most plentiful commodity and three dollars worth of it was often paid for a watermelon, seven dollars for an onion (!) and a similar price for a quart of potatoes. To this day vegetables are far scarcer than fruit.

CHAPTER XVI

THE LICK OBSERVATORY

WHY San José should be known pre-eminently as the Garden City in this land of gardens, or why it should wear that distinctive title was not quite clear to our minds until we remembered it received this christening before Pasadena was born, and also until we saw this productive Santa Clara valley where, it is estimated, there are more fruit orchards than in any other county of equal area in the republic. It is also a great centre for strawberries, and for vegetables of all kinds; indeed, the land for miles around is one vast garden.

The road leading thither from San Francisco runs through a fertile territory now in its fairest dress, the cultivated fields climbing far up the hillsides, the young grain making delicate shades of contrast in the chromatic scale of green, while near at hand our course passes through extensive olive and almond groves. Cherry orchards also abound, their leaves so lusty in size and thickness, the trees so altered in manner of growth by early and systematic pruning, from the scraggy shapes we remember that they almost defy recognition.

The city of San José (pronounced San Hosay) has numerous attractions, and is regarded as the Yankee town of the West, so many Eastern people having settled here. It was founded Nov. 29, 1777, by 15 people, and was once for a short time, the capital of the state. It is now an educational centre, the State Normal School occupying here 27 acres of lawn and flowers, with roses in fullest bloom climbing its brick walls. Located here also are the Santa Clara (Catholic) College, the Convent of Notre Dame, and the University of the Pacific. Business also thrives and it is proposed eventually to cut a canal through to this point, to advance the commercial interests of this fruitful region by giving increased outlet for its valuable products. We heard the usual story of one potato that was dug in this vicinity, which made further excavation unnecessary for the cellar of the house erected on its site, and as California houses very rarely possess a cellar of any description, we gave ready credence to the flattering tale. As a rule, both potatoes and apples are here inferior to those grown on Eastern farms.

The visitor to San José receives the welcome of an expected guest at the Hotel Vendome which though smaller than other noted hostelries of this state, is perhaps thereby the more cheery and home-like. One feels on entering as if he had always lived there and was in no haste to move on. This home-like atmosphere, impossible to describe, but so potently sensed, is still further enhanced by a natural environment which is charming and restful. The hotel, which is a handsome building of modified Gothic architecture, its façade divided by projections into five sections, edged by broad verandas, sits in a pretty park where the sun plays hide and seek with the shadows which the trees cast on the velvet lawn, while the air is soft and balmy as June. The tree trunks are covered to the upper branches with a thick green mass of clinging ivy, and at their base, seats are placed to enhance the comfort of the loiterer.

There are delightful drives in this vicinity, one to the Willows, a resort named for the trees which here abound in a beauty and luxuriance of foliage, a richness of emerald tint, an airy grace in the carriage of their flowing draperies which we have never seen them wear before. There is also the suburb of Santa Clara with its ancient mission, reached by a shady drive through the Alameda, which is Spanish for a road bordered by tall trees.

But the chief attraction of San José is of course Mount Hamilton with the Lick Observatory upon its summit, and a visit thither is an experience unique and delightful beyond description, a pleasure never thereafter to be forgotten.

Money is an excellent commodity, if its possessor owns with it a generous heart and an unselfish desire to benefit humanity. In various sections of this neighborhood we have met evidences of James Lick's benevolence, but his greatest gift, the crowning act of his life was the bequest of $700,000 for this valuable contribution to modern science. In his early life, while accumulating in So. America the nucleus of his large fortune, he became associated with a Spanish priest who in their out-door life, deeply interested the prospective millionaire in the study of astronomy, and then and there was formed in the mind of this reticent young man, the resolve to provide hitherto unparalleled advantages for the advancement of this noble science. It may be that his most eccentric economy had this noble end in view, as indeed that early disappointment, in his only *affaire du cœur* with the miller's daughter, was conducive to an unencumbered estate, with whose disposal no legal claimant could interfere.

Mount Hamilton is situated between two ridges of the Coast range, in a locality and at an altitude most favorable for observation and study of the heavens. To mount to its summit and descend in one day and night, usually conveys to the tourist an idea of excessive fatigue, and people are often slaves to their expectations. They saturate their minds with thoughts of weariness, place anxious sentinels on the outposts of their consciousness to watch for its first approach, and these fears are consequently realized. Those travellers, on the contrary, who are so in harmony with Nature that her grand and beautiful lessons serve as a perpetual tonic, filling the mind so full of gladness that it cannot hold thoughts of physical suffering, happily escape this painful bondage. The ascent of Mt. Hamilton is one prolonged feast of enjoyment, and a constant surprise. We had heard that the road which winds its tortuous course along these mountain ridges had been built at the expense of $80,000 and seven years of time, that it was macadamized all the way, and was everywhere wide enough for the passage of two teams, but we were not prepared to rise to an altitude of 4,448 feet without ascending even one hill, without climbing even one steep grade where the strained muscles and panting struggles of our four horses should make painful draughts upon our sympathies. Everything unpleasant is eliminated from this most perfect mountain drive.

Starting at noon from San José and reaching its suburbs, we gradually wind about the lowest foothills and along their slopes, rising at times about six feet in one hundred until this beautiful Santa Clara valley is unrolled beneath us like a rare mosaic of brilliant color and graceful outline. The fields are thickly dotted with flowers, the California poppy predominating; Flower of Gold, the Mexicans called it, known to our Eastern gardens as Escholtzia, from a General bearing that name, who landed at Monterey on the first ship which entered that bay. But in our small cultivated clumps we cannot catch the satiny sheen which forms a chief charm in the masses of these flowers which the wind sweeps over. As we ascended, the type of wild flowers changed, each family true to its own habitat, rarely found above or below its own chosen limits, and mostly new acquaintances in the floral kingdom, though we recognized varieties of delphinium, and of cyclamen.

While still enjoying this beautiful valley view, a sudden turn in our winding course hides it from sight and we see it no more. Neither is that white dome on the far distant summit which is our goal, any longer visible. A city set on a hill *can* be hid by more adjacent peaks, and for a long hour we are hemmed in by gorges and wooded heights that afford a constant variety of wild and romantic scenery until Smith's Creek is reached, where a little mountain inn provides refreshment for the hungry traveller. From this point the Observatory, which seems to withdraw itself farther and farther away as we pursue, is in an almost perpendicular position above us, and still seven miles away, but easily and gracefully that marvellous road curves round and round across the face of the mountain like a piece of serpentine braid, until nearer the summit it encircles the height three times, and even on the final grade reaches only the incline of thirteen feet to a hundred.

We drove up to the door of this imposing temple of science just before seven, in time to see a glorious sunset, and to catch its reflection from San Francisco Bay, miles to the north of us. Still farther northward on a clear winter's morning, Mt. Shasta is visible, as well as other kingdoms of this world and the glory of them. The visitor to the Observatory can always be sure of a hospitable welcome and painstaking effort for his entertainment, even though the kind hosts must find it wearisome to answer the same queries and repeat so often the same explanations and information.

Saturday evening is set apart each week as the only opportunity for the public to gaze through the great 36-inch telescope, hitherto the largest in the world, though we hear its bigger brother is even now in the skillful hands of the Messrs. Clark. To have reception night happen on the first quarter of the moon, (the most favorable time for observation) and under a perfectly clear sky was our rare good fortune. Passing from the vestibule, we entered the large dome with a feeling of awe, as if we stood in the presence of royalty, for towering far above us was the monster steel tube with its giant eye poised aloft, scanning searchingly the mysteries of unfathomed space. We could not help also a feeling of neighborly kinship for the glass which by some occult and mysterious method reached such perfection in distant Cambridge, away down there at the foot of Brookline street, where the crooked Charles, in uncertain mood flows both ways, lapsing lazily back and forth in its allegiance to the sea. We even congratulated this most-worshipful-grand-master lens on having exchanged the pungent marsh odor of that locality for the pure ether of this heaven-kissed height.

Wonderful was it to see the mammoth dome revolve with such ease under the direction of the presiding genii of the place, who with skillful touch also directed the telescope toward our satellite which held that evening high court in heaven. And how did it look? Well, very like its photograph, with much the unnatural whiteness and flowery appearance of plaster-of-paris, honey-combed as it is with volcanic craters. We, of course, improved this auspicious occasion to look intently for the man in the moon, but it must have been his night out, for we failed to discover him.

Leaving this lunar audience chamber we descended to the crypt below, where is the machinery which under hydraulic pressure furnishes the power to move the dome. It was a gruesome place, its darkness only partially penetrated by our one lantern, and here, in the massive brick masonry which supports the telescope and dome, is the tomb of James Lick. Strange mausoleum; a resting-place austere, peculiar and unique as was his life, but what more fitting monument than this princely instrument which rises from his breast, the culmination of a life-long purpose, like the aloe's mighty stem which blossoms late, but overtops all lowlier growths. Shall not this king of telescopes serve also as cenotaph for another noble man and devotee of science, even that revered son of Cambridge — Alvan Clark?

We next visited the smaller dome where the 12-inch telescope was focused upon the planet Saturn, and the kind and patient professor gave a running commentary on all the marvels which we saw. Most beautiful of all the heavenly bodies, especially serene fair Saturn seemed to-night with six of her attendant moons visible, and her golden rings casting deep shadows upon the planet, from the light of that same sun which also outlined the mountain peaks upon the moon's surface, and which we had seen disappear so recently from our horizon, although we caught its last luminous beams from the roof of this observatory, the highest point we have ever reached. The building is constructed with double walls of brick to secure evenness of temperature, and the bricks were made from a clay bed found fortunately near the summit.

Other wonderful instruments here abound. There are comet-seekers, earthquake-recorders, the transit instrument, which furnishes that uncertain quantity — time, for the whole Pacific coast, as far east as Ogden; there is the delicate Meridian Circle instrument for determining the latitude and longitude of stars, and many more. We listened with breathless interest to our young chaperon's delineation of these marvels, we nodded (we hope) in all the right places, and dragons shall never draw from us the confession whether or not our intelligent comprehension of their intricate mechanism is perfect and complete. Photography is also a feature here, and the long corridors are lined with most interesting solar and planetary views.

When at last our visit to this enchanting place was ended and we stood on the broad door-stone ready for departure, can we ever forget the scene outspread before us? Above, the wide expanse of star-lit heavens, though from our lofty perch it seemed less above us than a part of us. At the horizon shy Mercury, so rarely seen by city residents, shone with ruddy glow accompanied by the paler lustre of our well-known Venus. Opposite, majestic Orion kept up his eternal chase after

Taurus, the Pleiades hung nearer the zenith, while the moon's gentle radiance silvered the whole atmosphere and the great world of mountain, valley, and forest, lying calm and silent at our feet; it outlined the path our descending course must take, and how merrily we bowled along its almost parallel terraces, turning 366 sharp curves under the trained eye and practiced hand of a driver in whom we placed implicit trust.

But how that road did hold out, to be sure! Leaving the summit at 8.30, stopping only once to change horses, alighting here for a brief midnight stroll, (and for a most congenial interview with the wayside dog) we beheld as we neared the valley a new scene of beauty, a sea of fog beneath us, which under the magical touch of moonlight, seemed a frozen sea of ice, the dark outlines of the foot-hills serving as capes and promontories around which the white billows had congealed. We could readily imagine that our charioteer had transported us to the North pole, (we thought we discerned one end of it from the lofty perch we had just left) but as we descended, fair Luna slowly drew a misty veil across her face, it thickened until we saw her no more, or the electric lights on the towers of San José. But terra firma was reached, and at 1 A. M. we entered the Vendome, where a delicious and dainty lunch awaited us, a refreshing sleep, after which we awoke, without a vestige of fatigue, to the calm beauty of Sabbath morning, and to the heartfelt thanksgiving that a new treasure was henceforth hung in memory's priceless gallery.

CHAPTER XVII

SANTA CRUZ—MONTEREY

THE narrow-gauge route, leading from San José to the city of the Holy Cross, runs through the Santa Cruz mountains, indeed at times through the bowels of the earth, long tunnels being a feature of this road, but for the major portion of the journey, the scenery is both grand and picturesque. We look skyward for the tops of the loftiest peaks, gaze down into wild gorges many feet below us, send quick glances into the cañons which we hurry by, and gain many charming perspectives both ahead and behind our winding path. The mountain slopes are at this time literally purple with the plentiful wild lilac which makes soft contrast with the fresh ferns and dark pines towering above them. From the valleys, narrow paths lead up to our level, made by the feet of burros who carry on their backs and sides huge loads of wood from the clearings below to the waiting freight cars.

Five miles this side of Santa Cruz the road skirts the edge of the Big Tree grove, and here we alight, for although these are not the noted big trees of the Mariposa and Calaveras groves, they are a most interesting group and well repay a visit, especially as they possess an historical association, being the old camping ground of Gen. Fremont, and the hollow base of one of these monarchs, which still bears his name, he for some time made his head-quarters.

The redwood tree is found from the Oregon line to the Santa Cruz mountains. North of these boundaries is the Oregon cedar, south of this point, the Monterey cypress is indigenous. The redwood's manner of growth is to send up a multitude of surrounding shoots which eventually unite with the parent stem whose great size is thus due to conglomeration. All stages of this process can be observed in a stroll through the twenty or more acres of this natural temple. The largest single tree, known as Giant, is some twenty feet in diameter, its height is 300 feet, and its circumference is paced by thirty-seven masculine strides. In one of the Three Sisters, standing side by side, a stove is placed for the use of picknickers to this resort, but a majority of the trees are not hollow, being still it would seem in the freshness of youth. Alone and apart from his fellows towers Daniel Webster, a single tree, but less interesting than the groups of trees which spring from one base. The finest of these bears the incongruous name of Col. Ingersoll's Cathedral and consists of eight central trunks, surrounded by ten smaller ones, all united to a point above the ground that makes a climb to some of their numerous intersections only moderately easy. Another group of brothers has received the name of Young Men's Christian Association, and one more recently christened is known as Pres. Harrison, in which his wife is quite as large as he, and little baby McKee stands close by. The foliage of the redwood is very like our hemlock, only that it is borne higher aloft. There is a pleasant and interesting undergrowth in the grove, including yellow violets, and a new variety of white violet, with deep crimson eyes.

The curving line of the Bay of Monterey is nearly duplicated by the mountain range 20 miles inland, and in this pleasant sunny strip of territory, Santa Cruz is situated. It is a quiet seacoast town, with pretty residences and gardens, and attractive shops which display shells, delicate mosses, and other treasures of the sea. There are two miles of beautiful beach within the city limits, and in the cliffs beyond, the first sculptor, Neptune has carved grottoes and natural bridges, which richly reward a drive thither, although this natural curiosity does not equal the beauty of La Jolla on the San Diego shore. Congress has been recently petitioned to provide a breakwater for this pleasant bay, that vessels may here find safe and commodious anchorage. On certain days a little steamer crosses from Santa Cruz to Monterey, but to skirt the coast's crescent outline by rail is a three hours' journey.

The lethargic little town of Monterey is the quaintest place we have visited since Santa Fé. It is one of the towns where we have to rouse ourselves occasionally to make sure we are not dreaming. The locality was first "discovered" in 1602, when Vizcaino landed here and took possession of the country in the name of Philip III. of Spain, naming it in honor of the Viceroy of Mexico, Gaspar de Zuniga, Count of Monterey, who was projector of this northern cruise. Over 160 years later, still prior to our birth as a nation, the hitherto unbroken silence of this primitive region was stirred by another inscription on history's page, the founding of the old Carmel Mission by Father Serra, president of the band of Franciscan missionaries. The mills of the gods grind slow, but with unerring purpose toward the advancement of the race and the survival of the fittest. So Monterey at last witnessed the Franciscan downfall, and eventually the first establishment in California of U. S. authority, Gen. Fremont flinging to the breeze in July, 1846, from a flag-staff still preserved, that emblem of progress and freedom, the stars and stripes. Many of Monterey's residents are still of Spanish blood and their homes bear that distinctive national type, many being built of adobe and in some instances surrounded by high walls, which roses clamber over. The old one-story Spanish theatre still stands, though now used as a storehouse.

Two miles beyond Monterey, upon a promontory of the bay, stands pine-shaded Pacific Grove, originally selected as the annual camp-ground of the Methodist-Episcopal conference, but so delightful did the site prove that a town of two square miles has since sprung up with hotels, schools, and a thriving population, greatly increased in summer by the anniversary exercises of various societies of all denominations.

But the tourist is not drawn to this locality by any of these attractions. He comes chiefly and solely to visit the Hotel del Monte, in comparison with which everything else sinks into insignificance. One approaches the description of this charming place with reluctance, realizing his utter inability to do it justice, the meagre inadequacy of the most unabridged vocabulary of adjectives to portray its loveliness. However free a rein be given to the reporter's superlative pen, exaggeration is still impossible. This world in itself known as Del Monte, is situated a mile and a quarter this side of Monterey in a natural forest of pines and live-oaks, this environment suggesting its name, the word *monte* in Spanish being applied to either forest or mountain, so that the title is literally Hotel of the Forest. The building alone is beautiful, with its wide rambling façade, its long annexes on either side with their gracefully curved connecting corridors, and makes with its floral surroundings, the fairest of pictures, when viewed in chance sections through some opening in the tree branches as we ramble through the grounds. Within, the hotel is far more cosy than a place of such vast extent is apt to be; its reading and writing-room might serve as a family library, its drawing-room is most inviting and restful. The dining-room is more imposing, being large enough to seat 500 people, and its table-service of white frosted silver, suitably engraved "El Monte,"— The Forest—is of the finest description. There is not an unpleasant room in the house, and everywhere an almost painful neatness prevails. And ah! what sleep comes to the traveller here! The nights are a blank, a refreshing plunge in Lethean oblivion until the birds with enticing call lure us to an early walk beneath the umbrageous shades which they have chosen to inhabit. The mockingbird is common here, also the blue jay with his jaunty comb.

Setting forth to explore these wondrous grounds, whose outer boundaries we may not hope to fathom, a wrong direction can hardly be taken, nor is there possibility for its attractions to become monotonous. There is everywhere such variety of charm, such novelty, brilliancy and beauty. The diversity of floral display has no limit. There are ribbon beds and borders where every separate plant has its hair parted exactly in the middle, and not an eyelash is suffered to grow astray. There are more tangled plats where brilliant effects are produced by masses of contrasting colors. There are places set apart exclusively for rose culture, others for camelia japonicas; in one bed we counted fifty different varieties of calceolaria, each one handsome enough to exhaust a dozen exclamation points, and there is one large section devoted entirely to the culture of cacti of all kinds, many of them displaying the oddest most oriental-looking blossoms. All of these 126 acres of cultivated garden are heightened in charm by intervening stretches of beautiful green lawn, by lofty trees wreathed with ivy garlands, and from whose branches green moss hangs pendant, while masses of flowering myrtle surround their base. A maze is planted in the ground, formed of tall cypress hedges, from which if the explorer ventures too far he is liable to call lustily for assistance in emerging. Another feature is a large lake, the "Laguna del Rey" (Lake of the King) with a pleasant drive about it, bordered all the way by shrubs and the silvery plumes of pampas-grass;

boats are also provided for the guest to float at will on these placid waters.

Space fails to enumerate all the attractions of this sylvan retreat, but among them, and one of the proper things to do is to take the Seventeen-mile Drive, a road that includes a succession of beautiful views, both inland and of the ocean, also a visit to Monterey, Pacific Grove and the Carmel Mission. Inspiring scenes all, but on returning to the winding, shady avenues of the Del Monte we experience a fresh delight which is almost a surprise that the place is so surpassingly lovely. Can anything else compare with it? Does anything like it exist on this planet? Can even Paradise be fairer? If so, we hope the angel of Life, whom men call Death, will not tarry too long.

CHAPTER XVIII

TO THE YO SEMITE

TO spend a season in California and not visit the valley of the Yo Semite is to witness the play of Hamlet with the omission of its title-role. To go or not to go? That was the question. It was an easy matter to decide, the trip seemed an easy thing to accomplish; the very affable agent of the Berenda route thither, at his office in San Francisco, makes of the journey by his glowing rhetoric an enjoyable pastime, he smooths every difficulty from the tourist's path, allows him to select the seat he prefers in the photographed stage-coach with its three spans of prancing steeds. He paints the scenery with masterly touch, portrays the unprecedented grandeur of the waterfalls after this winter of unusual severity, unblushingly declares the existence of new cataracts, and other remarkable features never known before in the memory of man, with other fictions of his fertile imagination which leaves our previous hesitancy and doubt as to the advisibility of so early a visit to the mountains without a leg to stand upon. If he had asked us to sign away our entire fortune we should not have demurred, and certainly the mere bagatelle of the ticket's compensation it was quite a condescension for him to relieve us of. The stage fare is only $50.00 for the round trip (a slight discount being made to Raymond and Whitcomb protégés); $7.00 more pays the railway transit to and from the stage terminus, and as to the slight incidentals — but let us herewith draw a veil.

The start is made from San Francisco at sunset on the Los Angeles train which however drops us at midnight on a side track at Berenda. The cessation of motion, with the noise and jerks of disconnecting the car arouses the traveller who after waiting an hour or two for something else to happen, lapses into uneasy slumber only to be again disturbed by the arrival of the engine which, with the customary snorting and explosive puffs, attaches itself to take us to Raymond, by which recent growth of the railroad, the stage route has been cheated of twenty miles.

From this point the tourist sacrifices all further personal choice of his comfort, or hours of rest and action. He is no longer a free agent. Foreordination and pre-destination absolute are the rules of his being, the only authority recognized in this locality being the supreme omnipotence of the Yo Semite Stage and Turnpike Company. It arranges his down-sitting and uprising and regulates his thoughts afar off, for no bullet is ever sped from the muzzle of a gun with surer aim, more unswerving purpose, or with much greater speed than the tourist is propelled in and out of that Valley. Especially is this true of the rising hour. Accordingly we must be up and dressed after our broken night, with every toilet detail finished by 6 A. M., when the matutinal appetite must also be on deck ready for action, for it is thenceforth necessary that the traveller eat his dollar's worth at irregularly appointed intervals.

Breakfast over, the *four*-horse stage drives up to receive its load and we eye it askance. We have heard from friends who had made prior visits to the Valley, of the comfortable stages used on this route, of their canopied tops that serve as much needed screen from the rays of California's sun. Earlier specimens of the genus stage may have been comfortable; we occupied one of a newer style. The canopy was there, in fact we made caput-al acquaintance with it at certain points in our ride quite as often as we tested the springs (?) of the seat. The stage had four seats, the back-seat upholstered with enamelled-cloth all the way down; the middle seat with its minimum amount of motion; the front seat, easier than the rear but with a restricted range of view; and the much coveted seat with the driver, hot and sunny but having the advantage of a wide spread landscape and the most entertaining conversation of the charioteer who is always a stuffed encyclopædia of information, of stories and legends, some of them perhaps having a shadowy foundation of truth. The drivers are as a rule careful, obliging and good-natured, all rules of course being marked by exceptions. The horses are well fed, well taken care of, are in good flesh despite their daily toil, and are frequently changed; they are all duly and appropriately christened, Type-setter, Pile-driver and Charley Ross being members of our team. The coaches — perhaps we mentioned these vehicles before but the subject is a fertile one — are strong and thoroughly well-made in their running gear, comfort being sacrificed here to substantiality, but their interior is crude, cheaply finished, with no provision even of straps suspended from its roof to steady the helpless passenger. A good smart Yankee would renovate these vehicles with many comfortable and helpful appurtenances. At present, they are most unbearable even when standing still.

But we load into this commodious lumber-wagon and set forth by a narrow circuitous mountain road, in an atmosphere radiant and redolent with purity, brilliancy and all sweet odors. The breath of the hills is blown to us, the blossoms of the valley waft upward their fragrance. Gradually we rise, winding round sloping hillsides, from whose vantage ground we look down into verdant fields and charming valleys. Unfamiliar wild flowers line the roadside with many old favorites including several varieties of lupin, blue and pink and white, the vermilion painted cup, and vivid mountain pink, large bushes of the wild white lilac, and of the buckeye bearing aloft their white panicles as do our horse chestnuts at home; and here also we made our first acquaintance with the mariposa lily, or butterfly tulip, in white and lemon and deep yellow with large brown spots on each of the three leaves forming its fragile cup.

On and still on we wind, soon gaining glimpses of snow-capped mountains so far away on the horizon that we cannot conceive our course includes those distant heights, that any route not threaded by steam could include so long a trip, but we learn that those misty summits comprise only the first "divide"; the first night of our journey being spent beyond those snowy peaks. At our second change of horses, we pass a quartz mill where the mountain has been tunnelled for the precious ore and the fair face of nature has been frequently scarred by the prospector's spade as he for a time follows a false lead. We pass the lively Fresno river and also an artificial log-flume built on tall trellises for 55 miles to convey timber from the wooded hills down to marketable levels. Some of the hills which we pass have a peculiar topography being ridged lengthwise by a series of undulating swells, divided by parallel hollows about 20 feet apart, as if the hillside had once served as a leviathan graveyard. At our fourth change of horses—Grant's Sulphur Springs—we stop to enjoy the generous lunch awaiting us, and a short rest.

Our afternoon's task is to climb by slow and painful degrees to the summit of Chow-chilla peak, near which as we reach it, a wonderful view is obtained of the San Joaquin valley, (the light sedge grass giving it the appearance of a vast desert), of the Coast range beyond, and of one little dark spot, so far away as to be almost invisible, which is pointed out as the Raymond we left — when? Can it be only *this* morning that we started, that but a half day has intervened between us and civilization, since the possibility was ours of occasionally looking upon a human habitation? But soon, nearer the height, we have a diverting novelty in the form of snow-drifts as high as the top of our coach, though the road-bed is bare.

The summit is reached joyfully, for now we begin the descent into the valley where our day's journey will end. But such a descent! The stage it seems is behind time, the driver's reputation must be preserved even at the expense of the necks or limbs of his passengers, and so the horses, breathless from their long hard pull, are given free rein, are not checked even at the murderous water-bars, or at the rough places where the wheels wallow in the soft mud to their hubs and the coach oscillates correspondingly. What matters it that the weary, worn, and sore human freight are thrown violently from side to side, or against the roof, until their necks are well-nigh dislocated, what if their breath is beaten from their bodies by severe and incessant jouncing, until the only thought of the hour is the promise of salvation to them who *endure unto the end*, with also the firm resolution if life is spared to reach home (which now seems doubtful) that we will advise everbody to postpone their visit to the Yo Semite until they get to heaven and can look down. We recall the remark of a dear lady who declared that she was never so near her Maker as when in the Valley. We certainly never expect to be so near Purgatory again as when on our journey thither. Other friends had assured us that the surrounding scenery as we rode along would make us forget every discomfort. The scenery is doubtless grand hereabouts, the monarchs of this forest among the noblest specimens we have ever seen. We remember gaining fugitive glimpses, as we came down to the seat occasionally, of several trees reeling and swaying across our spasmodic vision like tipsy revellers, but we neglected to speak of them, knowing our tongues would be severed in the attempt. We shall long remember the descent of Chow-chilla as a needless outrage perpetrated upon innocent victims. But our discomforts safely ended at nightfall when we drove up to the Wawona Hotel to receive the courteous attention, the cleanly rooms, and excellent table always provided by those excellent men, the Washburn brothers. The wonder is to find anything to eat so far away from market, or depot.

The sleep of the righteous visits every pillow at Wawona, a baptism of health and strength likewise descends as if from the mountains that surround on every side this cup-like vale, the alchemy of this rare elixir sweetens the sorely-tried disposition of the disgusted traveller and (as a natural consequence) restores to freshness the storm-tossed frame. What luxury it would be to lie in the early dew-fragrant dawn and let the restfulness and calm soak in to one's consciousness but— we are bought with a price and our purchasers are *pro tem.* our masters. We must therefore be awakened at five, breakfast at six, and with dread and trembling mount another coach for the drive thence into the Valley where we are due at 2 P.M. Will it, at last, we wonder compensate us for all this misery? We have ceased to ask regarding distances, for miles mean nothing here.

Among the fictions of the trip is the statement that the stage-ride is one of sixty miles. Invert the six to approach nearer the truth. And how do they measure miles in these mountains? We learned this from our truthful (?) driver. A pack of grayhounds are loosed and allowed to run until they drop dead from exhaustion, at which point the first mile stake is placed, a fact which no visitor to the Valley can ever gainsay.

But the ride of to-day is a great improvement upon that of yesterday. Our driver is careful and compassionate, the road is in better condition and the scenery is much grander and less monotonous. Following for a time the south fork of the Merced, we begin to wind about and ascend the last barrier which lies between us and our goal, reaching a height of over 6000 feet, gaining along the way, from Lookout and other points, wild grand views of deep gorges far, far below us through which the winding river cuts its way between the mountains. Around us is an almost unbroken forest of sugar pine, and yellow pine with its alligator-leather trunk, while every dead branch and twig is swathed with moss of living green, so kindly does our mother Nature heal every wound, and transform death into beautiful life. Light growths are few, though it is still early for flowers and ferns, but we see an occasional specimen of the wonderful crimson snow-plant. The

Manzanita hangs full of pinkish waxen blossoms, its branches so twisted and crooked that every bush is searched in vain for a stem straight enough to serve as a cane. This wood works up very beautifully for ornamental veneering.

At our second change of horses about noon, we take the opportunity to run down the road ahead of the coach, for a restful change, we inspect the watering trough, the road, the trees which here allow such restricted range of view, when, speeding on lest the fresh horses overtake us too soon, suddenly, as if the planet had dropped from beneath our feet, the trees disappeared on our right, the sky rolled itself backward like a scroll to give space to a vast army of peaks and domes and mountains of granite, a double row, the verdant gorge between, and we realized with a gasp that was almost pain, that we were looking upon the marvellous Valley. We stood on Inspiration Point.

Majestic, solemn, awe-some in the massive sweep of its gigantic contours, in the wonderful stillness, the immovable calm that broods above it, as if here it was that God rested "on the seventh day from all that He had created and made, the heavens and all the host of them." There are some moments, some experiences that come to us which are untranslatable in any human speech, and this was one. Stirred to the innermost depths of our being, where reverence and humility stand side by side, we resolved, realizing our impotence, never to commit the sacrilege of attempting to describe this master-piece of the Creator, and we never will. Let it be written alone on tables of stone.

How long we might have stood there had not the coach arrived to pick us up, we cannot say. The driver kindly dissected the grand spectacle for us, letting us down easily to ordinary levels of thought and feeling, and explained that the massive buttress on the left was El Capitan; on our right were the Three Graces, in the farthest distance, the North, and South or Half-Dome, as if our stunned and bewildered consciousness could take cognizance of compass-points; over there was Cloud's Rest, so-called because clouds often hover upon it when other spots in the Valley are clear. The white ribbon let down several hundred feet from one of these heights is we learn Bridal Veil Fall, only to be enjoyed from a nearer view where its misty drapery floats airily and gracefully as the wayward zephyrs frolic with its gossamer meshes, and especially when the afternoon sun-beams, flooding it with their prismatic dyes, make of it a vision of loveliness too fair for earth. A smaller fall high up on the mountain's face is disrespectfully known as "The Widow's Tear" because, being supplied by melting snows, it dries up in six weeks. On the opposite side of the Cañon are Cascade falls, and the delicate pleasing Ribbon fall, such airs and graces do these stern ledges assume, such beauty do they clothe themselves withal. This lightness tempers somewhat, as does this minute particularization of these varied features, the deep emotion, the painful tension which the sublimity and grandeur of the scene inspires. Never again do we expect to read so clearly in terrestrial language the mighty impress of the Almighty Hano, the tracing of the Infinite Sculptor. It was with a positive relief at last that we turned our backs upon the mighty gorge and followed the serpentine trail down the last steep slope to the Valley's floor. A seven-mile drive still lay between us and the hospitable doors of the Stoneman House, but with its genial proprietor, Mr. J. J. Cook, as fellow-passenger, we were naturally in no undue haste to end our journey.

What a drive it was! What a revelation of our own insignificance, of our utter incapacity to take in such immensity with the faintest approach to due appreciation, or the folly of attempting to adapt our little two-foot rule of measurement to this gigantic scale. For instance, the driver pauses to point out a minute green twig just above a heap of talus, on the side of El Capitan. After careful inspection we at last discern something which might serve as a doll's Christmas tree, whereupon we are asked to believe that by actual measurement the tree is 125 feet high. We stop again to admire the grand old Sentinel, the majestic Cathedral Spires, pausing longest at the foot of the Bridal Veil whose cool breath suggested to the Indian the baleful influence of an evil spirit, Po-ho-no, which name was given to this vision of indescribable beauty. The cataract feeds three streams which here seek the river, the beautiful river of Mercy (Merced) which, flowing through its entire length, is not the least charm of the Valley. Indeed were it not for this clear, limpid stream, and the beautiful green meadows with which it surrounds itself, the rich growth which it feeds, the austere and massive grandeur of the Valley would be well-nigh unbearable.

As it is, the first mental impression and one not lifted until the second day, is that of overwhelming sadness. The burden of isolation oppresses us. Heaven itself is not so far away as are we from every mundane interest or association. If these stern gray ledges were not *quite* so high, if their magnificent proportions could be toned down just a little nearer our comprehension, if the cataracts were less tremendous in their daring leaps.

Ah verily, what is man that Thou art mindful of Him, or the son of man that Thou visitest him with such revelation of Thy matchless glory, Thy Creative Majesty?

CHAPTER XIX

IN THE VALLEY

THE location of the pretty Stoneman House, built by the State, is well chosen. Almost the entire length of the Valley must be threaded to reach it, and when there, the visitor is surrounded by most attractive points of interest. On the left, Glacier point rises 7000 feet; on the right are the Royal Arches and Washington Tower, while the grand Yo Semite fall makes its three gigantic leaps apparently but a stone's throw distant, although if one wishes to make nearer acquaintance with its varied phases of beauty and decides to stroll down the road until he comes opposite to this mighty cataract, he will continue to stroll for some time and approach no nearer to its base than when it proved such an irresistible magnet from his seat on the hotel veranda. A beautiful view can be obtained from the rear of Barnard's hotel, and at this point the majestic roar, with the bomb-like explosions peculiar to this fall are constantly heard. It is a fascination of which one never tires to watch this ceaseless motion, this never-wearied activity, which approaches the Goethean ideal of "unhasting, unresting," for in all these cataracts and cascades there is a suggestion of laziness in their descent, until one remembers the unrealizable height which their waters span. They seem in no hurry to leave those solemn heights and join the chattering river, they indulge in little side-escapades, shoot out a rocket here and there, take time to clothe their watery sheen with concealing mists and vapors, but the great heart within beats in true rhythm to Nature's mighty laws, and the key-note of their grand symphony is in ascending scale like the "Hallelujah" chorus: "For the Lord God Omnipotent reigneth."

On the hither side of the Yo Semite is the Indian Cañon up whose steep sides and rocky débris the Yo Semite tribe escaped when pursued by the Mariposa recruits, in May 1851, on the occasion of the first entrance to the valley of any white man. The depth of this defile, its rough and jagged features are wonderfully revealed when the morning sun manages to smuggle a few of his gilded beams into the wild gorge. In winter the Valley's allowance of sunlight is but two hours long. The name Yo Semite, as is well known, signifies a great grizzly bear, not from any resemblance which the gorge bears to this animal, but because of a successful encounter in prehistoric times, of a young chief with one of these monsters, whom the athlete slew, though unarmed, save with the dead limb of a tree. To perpetuate this deed of prowess, the name of the animal was given as a title of honor to the young brave, was transmitted to his children, and thus eventually to the tribe which occupied the valley when it was discovered.

Speaking of sunrises reminds every Valley visitor at once of the marvellous experience at Mirror lake. It is doubtful if anywhere on the planet there is a lovelier spot than this crystal sheet of liquid purity, at the base of Mt. Watkins especially in the early dawn when it is still, as the Indians called it, a "sleeping water," and not a ripple has as yet disturbed its dreamless rest. It is a visible expression of

> "The peace at the heart of Nature,
> The light that is not of day."

Clear-cut as a cameo, the mighty peaks penetrate these watery depths, 4000 to 6000 feet below us, their scars and clefts repeating themselves with such startling vividness that effects not noticeable through the medium of the air are plainly discerned through the limpid wave. Some discolorations on a crag a mile perhaps above us are a train of cars and engine in that illusive nether world. A clothes-line with the washing all hung out so early in the morning, is the most realistic thing imaginable. Entranced we stand on the margin of this crystal floor watching the marvellous picture, noting its soft contrasts of light and shade play about those gigantic cliffs beneath that wondrous distant sky; we gaze longingly as an exiled Peri might stand outside the gates of Paradise, and yearn in vain to enter. But now a wonderful scene opens. A faint flush glorifies the world at our feet, a golden dart pierces its azure calm, another of roseate hue thrills and warms the scene, gilding each massive outline with a luminous halo, and now quicker and faster the radiant beams shoot over the slopes of yon granite mountain in the nadir realm, until the first curve of the great luminary is seen, higher and higher it mounts till the sun has gloriously risen and dimmed that enchanted world whose denizens we were. Again and again, as we seek a new position on the mirror's edge, is the scene repeated, while we resolutely turn the back of our head toward the zenith where one generally looks for solar displays, and gaze down, down thousands of feet, it would seem, into the visionary and unreal. How like it is to our mortal experience, where the reflection is all that our dull eyes discern, where we turn constantly away from the real and the true, the life that is spirit, for the glamour of its shadow, which must ever fade from our perception, as the Sun of

Truth dawns upon our spiritual consciousness.

The trips which can be made in the Valley are legion, and a week, at least should be devoted to them, though in this connection it might be well to advise the tourist to "put money in his purse" for to quote from a witty commentator, "Man brought nothing into this world, and if he stays long in the Yo Semite Valley, it is certain he will carry nothing out." All that the hotels and Stage Co. do not get, the wily livery man will. The trails to Glacier Point, Eagle Peak and Upper Yo Semite are at the date of our early visit not yet open (the emphatic ten-days-old statement of the affable agent in San Francisco to the contrary, notwithstanding), but the most satisfactory and beautiful of all the excursions (we speak necessarily from limited experience) is that to Vernal and Nevada falls.

The trail from Tis-sa-ack bridge along Grizzly Peak, though hewn out of solid rock is almost wide enough for a carriage, and yet our well-trained steed prefers a footing so close to the edge that we seem to hang far over the steep precipice, but we do not demur. We remember that he knows far more about his business than we ever shall, and that if we are born to be hung or drowned we cannot possibly suffer harm on this winding stair. The Mohammedan fatalism would really be an excellent travelling companion, or rather that *perfect* trust which casteth out *every* fear, and never under any circumstances knows a shadow of trembling. In entering this grand cañon, we leave the Yo Semite behind, having Glacier Pt. one of its boundaries, at our back, the beautiful little Illilouette fall high up towards the clouds on our right, towering ledges on either side, and at their base the main current of the Merced river struggling over its rocky bed. We soon approach a bridge spanning the noisy stream and turning to cross it, that vision of beauty, the Vernal fall bursts suddenly, dazzlingly upon our view in the near distance, and takes our most ardent expectancy by surprise. Gladly we dismount at Register rock and clamber over and around moist boulders to approach nearer the foot of this crystal torrent as far as Lady Franklin Rock to which point, in 1863, that lady was carried in a chair. The Fall is not very hospitable in its welcome, it will not allow us to reach the "ladders" by which it is possible to climb to its highest level, for it drenches us and drives us back by a spray so dense as to be blinding and almost suffocating.

Returning, we again mount and thread a zig-zag trail backward, forward, and upward, this equestrian procession forming three or four tiers across the face of the mountain, each row being far above the next lower, when at last reaching the highest point, in a twinkling that takes one's breath away, the marvellous grandeur of the Nevada fall, and that handsome dome, the Cap of Liberty, bursts at once upon our enraptured gaze. There is something very imposing about this isolated height. It is unique and singular, both in shape and characteristics. It appeals strongly to the appreciation of the beholder, and aroused in us a far deeper emotion than did El Capitan; we could never tire of studying its grand proportions. We turn aside here to visit the top of the Vernal fall, where leaning over a huge stone buttress, a natural balustrade, we look adown its wide expanse of emerald water and diamond spray tangled and broken into rainbows far below, a scene never to be forgotten. The river here is wonderful in its mad haste, its cascades and whorls and wild upward tossings, its Silver Aprons and Emerald Pools. We followed the course upward, our beauty-loving hearts unable to absorb fast enough the wealth of varied grandeur that surrounds us, until we reach the foot of Nevada fall, an appropriate climax to a day on which we have touched tide-water of rarest enjoyment.

Beautiful beyond suggestion, grandest, most fascinating object in all the Valley, we could sit for hours and watch its changeful flow. The whole Merced river here falls over a mountain wall 617 feet high, although the water seems less to fall than to resolve itself into froth and foam, and float out upon the air, to wave silvery banners here and there and then pierce them with flying rockets, so rarely repeating the same effects that the observer appreciates the appropriateness of the Indian title which means "meandering," though this is the last word one would expect to find in a savage vocabulary.

> "Now shining and twining,
> And pouring and roaring,
> And glittering and frittering,
> And gathering and feathering,
> And whitening and brightening,
> And quivering and shivering,
> And dashing and flashing and splashing and clashing,
> And so never ending, but always descending,
> Sounds and motions forever and ever are blending,
> All at once and all o'er, with a mighty uproar,
> And this way the water comes down at Lodore."

A house has sprung up here (Snow's), we hardly know how, unless it grew through a new law of evolution peculiar to this land of wonders. It was not yet open, so we spread our lunch upon an adjacent rock and quaffed nectar from the clouds, feasting our eyes meanwhile (the truest refreshment) on that lovely veil of silver sheen, suspended across the mountain's breast, on whose enchanting grace we hope sometime again to look.

Morning in the Yo Semite Valley! What a rare experience to return from the realm of spirit and take up again our physical instrument amid such sublimity of environment, to renew once more our conscious connection with the material world within the hidden fastnesses of these eternal hills! What a solemn hour it should prove, what new baptism it must impart, to strengthen the soul for all sterner duties which await us! *Is* the hour such? Alas, no; repose is an unknown quantity in this region. Even the border land of dream-life is invaded by the hurrying and skurrying of departing guests, and when at last our time arrives, the porter's prompt reveille upon our door puts a speedy end to contemplation, or devotion. At no stage of the Yo Semite trip is an early departure less imperative than for the drive from the Stoneman House to Wawona, consequently with strange masculine inconsistency, the hour fixed by the "Turnpike" Medes and Persians is the earliest of them all. At quarter of six, with valises packed, and breakfast bolted, our four-horse team (Star and Keno, Girl and Sullivan, who lacks as yet the diamond belt of his godfather) stand pawing the ground at the door. We mount and hurry down the Valley, striving to impress indelibly upon our memories its every feature, we pass from its portals, climb again to the summit, jounce down the other side, and reach Wawona at one. The mid-day repast is immediately served and without a moment's opportunity even for customary ablutions, we are loaded into an open vehicle, far easier than the stage however, and are driven away to the Mariposa grove of Big Trees, a spot we have longed to visit, but the Frost King having prolonged his reign to this unprecedented date, the snow still lies too deep for the customary drive through the excavated heart of the living tree, Wawona. The Grizzly Giant, claimed to be the largest tree in the world, is 33 feet in diameter and nearly 100 in circumference. Standing against its mammoth proportions the plumpest person in our party looked a child, this being the only way to assist the eye to a true measurement and realization of the tree's enormous size.

These *Sequoia gigantea* are a slightly different species from the redwood of the Santa Cruz region, which are classified as the *Sequoia sempervirens*. Their generic name was chosen to perpetuate the memory of Sequoyah, a Cherokee chieftain of remarkably advanced mind, he having invented an alphabet of eighty-six characters that his tribe might have a written language, the system being still in use. Our national heroes are duly remembered in the christening of the grove, with some of our scientists and poets. One tree known as the Telescope, allows a range of vision 125 feet upwards, its hollow trunk having been burned out, but sap enough still flows through the shell to support foliage. Many of the trees are thus marked by the ravages of fire. The grove is not composed wholly of these giant trees, the growth being chiefly of different varieties of pine, whose size elsewhere would seem worthy of note, and the showy white blossoms of the dog-wood are also plentiful.

The succeeding night is spent at Wawona, a place with attractions of its own, the beautiful Chil-noo-al-na falls being near by, with other pleasant mountain excursions. The studio of Thomas Hill located here is an interesting place to visit, its gallery of art-treasures being freely open to all. The return journey to Raymond held less of the terrors which beset our entrance to this mountain pass, for the road had been put in excellent order by the faithful efforts of the road-commissioners aided by the warm dry breath of old Sol. But he was a little too ardent in his glances that afternoon. The heat for many long hours was intolerable, we had a foretaste of the dust which smothers the tourist of a later date, and when at twilight the Raymond inn dawned upon our horizon, with some real Pullman cars awaiting us near by, the sentiment of the party could only vent itself in the devout doxology "Praise God from whom all blessings flow."

One of the most graceful things ever said of the Yo Semite was inscribed on the hotel register by James Vick, whose name is enshrined in the heart of all flower-lovers the country over. "The road to Yo Semite, like the way of life, is narrow and difficult, but the end, like the end of a well-spent life, is glorious beyond the highest anticipation." But far more practical is the declaration of Hon. Thomas Scott of the Penn. Central R.R. "If my business interests lay upon this coast, I would build a railroad to this truly marvellous valley within one year from this date."

This truly is the need of the hour. The "marvellous valley" is too far away. Candor compels us to confess (for we "cannot tell a lie") that the trip thither is the most inhuman experience in the world. With a railway built even half way to its ponderous doors, the Cañon of the Great Grizzly Bear must long remain the Mecca of every traveler, the shrine at which all devotees of Nature will reverently bow.

CHAPTER XX

HOMEWARD BOUND

WHAT a glorious journey it is to sweep across our American continent from the Pacific coast to Atlantic shores, to climb over two mighty mountain ranges, cross a wide desert, to skirt the borders of inland seas both salt and fresh, to be ferried over rapidly-coursing rivers by boat or bridge, to whiz along prairies that are granaries vast enough for a world's supply, to cross thus a galaxy of states and territories with a portion also of Her British Majesty's dominions, and to enjoy all this from the luxurious environment of a palace-car, where choice viands are served with clock-like regularity, — what a rich experience it is! Can one ever realize the tremendous extent of this country, or its wonderful resources, its mineral and agricultural wealth until he views it thus from shore to shore? And when to other comforts is added the Raymond espionage which means the absence of all care as to the detail of the long journey, when with a vigilance that neither slumbers nor sleeps the "ubiquitous Lyon" numbereth his wayward flock by name and suffereth not a trunk to go astray without his watchful notice, with what peace we lay us down and sleep, only to wake to the lightness and freedom of another halcyon day.

A possibly envious friend once said teasingly "no one who has any brains ever travels with the Raymonds", recognizing thus the freedom from anxious personal supervision which such excursionist enjoys. Blessed then are the brainless ones, or those who having used their brains to good purpose have earned now the right to such reposeful recreation. Brains do not lie fallow while travelling. Plentiful opportunities occur for storing the mind with valuable information, every hour suggesting new thought, broadening the range of mental vision, which is all the clearer because not absorbed in petty cares concerning that which is least.

On a warm sunshiny afternoon near the close of May 1890, after a long and delightful sojourn in this fair Western land, we at last with great reluctance turn away from the Golden Gate and set our faces eastward. The calm blue waters of the bay seem loth to ripple their last farewell, for through inlet and cove they merge into San Pablo bay and thence to Napa creek, where Vallejo is seen four miles away, opposite to Mare island, an important western naval station, a verdant spot, a rendezvous for roses and trailing vines and leafy shades which embower the officers' pleasant homes and make brilliant the hospital grounds. In the stream near by is anchored Admiral Farragut's flag-ship, the Hartford, disabled now and roofed over to prevent further ravages of the elements.

At this point we reach Port Costa and our course changes for before we are aware our entire train with one other and their two powerful engines are quietly transferred to the largest ferry-boat in the world — the Solano. Of course every one is on deck at once, for who ever knew a Raymond tourist to remain in his own car one moment after it became stationary, although with equal alacrity he melts from sight like the dew in his obedient response to the first call "all aboard." Some twenty minutes are consumed in crossing the Straits of Carquinez, and at Benicia we resume our long landward journey, until at dusk we reach California's capital — Sacramento — where our accommodating intinerary allows us a stop-over of a night and half-day.

In only eight instances in our Republic is the capital of a state its metropolis and the capital of California is not its most attractive city. The portion devoted to residences is charming, and great attention is paid to floral adornment. We have never seen magnolia trees in fuller wealth of bloom than they here display, and contrasting with them is the bright green foliage and vivid pink of the pomegranate. Broad streets intersect each other at right angles but the main business portion of the city wears an old-time look, which bespeaks its record of mining days, the early rendezvous as it was of westward bound emigrants, the first settlement to greet the eyes of weary wanderers over the plains. Many of the buildings are still Mexican in type, with broad verandas across their second story, and bearing the marks of age and delapidation. The sidewalks are of wood, and so much raised above the street level as to require a bridge of sharp descent and ascent at each street corner. Cleanliness is not a feature of this part of the city, however noticeable in more favored localities.

The Capitol building sits grandly in its beautiful park and leaves nothing to be desired in its architecture or ornamentation. Its senate-chamber and assembly hall contain full length portraits of California's governors, the corridors and stairways are adorned with paintings illustrating early scenes in the phenomenal history of the state, while in the rotunda on the first floor is seen that notable piece of statuary, Columbus before Isabella, these two figures of heroic size, together with the kneeling page of the Queen, being carved from one solid block of marble by Larkin G. Mead, and presented by D. G. Mills to the

State of California. As we gaze admiringly upon this work of art we cannot restrain the wish that the fair Isabella could have foreseen the magnitude of the cause to which she pledged her jewels, or the marvellous growth which would spring from that tiny seedling planted by her hopeful hand; that her woman's soul could have seen its faith justified, and have read her own record in the history of nations, could have known that she would be thus immortalized, sitting here enthroned in this marble paved temple with the warm golden light from its open portals touching her face and form with a glory that is almost life.

Art has in Sacramento another chosen home. A valuable collection has been donated by Mrs. Charles B. Crocker, who also built in her own grounds the handsome building which holds these treasures of painting and sculpture. The many rare gems which are here so attractively placed would require more time to properly appreciate and enjoy than we have at our command, but we still carry away many delightful remembrances to enrich future thought. In the position of honor in the main hall, beneath a massive painting of Yo Semite, rests the tie of California laurel and four iron rails which formed with the golden spike the last connecting links in that narrow shining bridge which spans a continent, to whose completion the efforts of Mr. Crocker lent such valuable assistance. It was at Promontory, near Ogden where the Central Pacific R. R. building east and the Union Pacific hastening westward finally met, May 10, 1869.

> "Where two Engines in our vision
> Once have met, without collision."

> "What was it, the Engines said
> Pilots touching — head to head,
> Facing on the single track
> Half a world behind each back?"

> "*What* it was the Engines said,
> Unreported and unread,
> Spoken slightly through the nose,
> With a whistle at the close,"

only Bret Harte heard, and translated for our duller comprehension and certainly no recent date has chronicled an event of greater importance, of vaster moment to the nation.

Leaving Sacramento at noon and threading the orchards and vineyards that encompass her about, passing beyond this smiling valley toward the foot hills where we view many traces of hydraulic mining (a method now forbidden by law, lest the hills themselves be washed away, and the lowlands become unfertile, the rivers unnavigable), we commence with keen anticipation the ascent by daylight of the Sierra Nevada mountains, two strong engines with labored breath attempting the upward grade.

If friends at home should try to mentally locate us now, probably the last point at which the wildest imagination could place us would be rounding Cape Horn; and yet this is the first experience we are called upon to enjoy. On a high promontory of the first range we ascend, a narrow shelf has been pecked away from the rocky heart of the mountain (at first by men suspended by ropes from the summit), now daily used as the main highway of this large railway system, and exactly on the sharpest curve of the cape we pause for some minutes in mid-air to enjoy the wondrous scene unrolled beneath us. Hundreds of feet below, a deep verdant gorge, through which the muddy American river winds like a tiny thread, wide and turbulent as it doubtless is, if true to its title, leading the eye by graceful twist and turn, out from these lofty confines to other chasms beyond. Turning from this dizzy height, we have just time to press the wild azaleas which find room to grow on this sterile point, when we stop for orders at Blue Cañon. And why "Blue"? Is the river that rises here bluer than other mountain streams, albeit the waters of the little brook are so clear and pure that we delightedly fill our drinking cups at its brim and gather the spearmint which borders its edge, or is the name given because of this bluish afternoon haze that floods both sides of the cañon, our track here as in many other places following the outline of the letters U and V and Z.

But just as we grow enthusiastic over these beautiful Sierra, rushing from side to side of the car in response to some neighbor's frantic appeal to "look," presto, change! and there comes a blank. Darkness profound hems us in, and the fact dawns upon us that we are in a snow shed; and we leave it only to enter another, and another, tunnel alternating with snow shed for over forty miles of oblivion. How tired we all grew as the hours wore on of the long eclipse, how aggravating to catch occasional glimpses, through cracks between the boards, of beautiful landscapes around us only to lose them before they were discerned. How cold was the breath of those deep snow drifts, some of them the accumulation it would seem of a score of years, how pityingly we recalled the sufferings of those poor travellers imprisoned here during last winter's blockade, how we shouted with relief and joy when at last the radiant sun streamed in upon us, just after the lovely Donner Lake, of saddest history had been passed. Soon after we reach Truckee, a rough little lumber town, where we are side-tracked, and after a ramble about the place, the inspection in its round-house of the giant rotary snow-plough which did such valiant service a few months ago (although but for those despised snow-sheds, the invention of

Mr. Crocker, and built at an average expense of $10,000 a mile, all the snow-ploughs in the world could not keep open that narrow mountain path), we are lulled to sleep by the splash and roar of Truckee's riotous river, and rest until the matin's peal of the "regular" train which arrives at daybreak, at whose heels we continue our journey.

CHAPTER XXI

SALT LAKE CITY

THE region between Truckee, the last town in California, and Reno, the first of note in Nevada is exceedingly picturesque. The eastern spurs of the Sierra still surround us, the merry little river, with its cascades and whirlpools and wild current which almost mock our speed, is our constant companion. Unlike most streams the Truckee is borne full grown as it flows only from the fresh water Lake Tahoe to the saline basin of Pyramid Lake, 97 miles distant, draining the one and supplying the other without altering the characteristics of either. While still revelling in its boisterous beauty, feeling the spirit of its frolic, a white post beside the track marks our passage of the State Line, and California is now behind us, our pleasant experience within its borders but a reminiscence.

Fair golden state, farewell! We turn our faces eastward and hasten away but we leave our hearts behind, oh gracious princess, to whom all wondrous gifts have been vouchsafed that thou in turn mayest lavish them upon each idle comer. Ours too forever are thy mountain chains, and verdant valleys, thy desolate gorges and fruit-laden, rose-smothered gardens, thine awful cañons, cataracts and winding rivers, desert, plain and city, all, all are ours in blessed memory. May the joys you have showered upon the strangers within your gates return upon you and yours a thousand-fold. We go reluctantly, still turning back to waft a warm farewell. Bill Nye says truly that while many go to California, but few return. We surmise also that not a few who do return resolve to go again at their earliest opportunity. A year's residence in this part of our Republic is well nigh fatal to one's allegiance to other localities, so potent and irresistible is California's subtle charm.

No greater contrast could be imagined than the scenery afforded by our first and second day's travel. When Reno and its pink sand-verbenas are left behind, we enter upon the desert and traverse its level wastes through the entire day and night, although even here the monotony is relieved by many interesting features. Snow-clad mountains are almost constantly in sight from a greater or less distance. Frequently along our course what seems to be a little dust-eddy, a cyclone in miniature, reveals the existence of boiling springs and their steaming escape-valves. At Humboldt, where we alight at noon, the arid soil has been converted into a refreshing little oasis of green grass and splashing fountain, and here, two Piute squaws bring to the station a much-swathed and basket-imprisoned pappoose who is further fettered by a cotton-cloth veil which can only be lifted to reveal the charms beneath on presentation, by the curious, of a nickel, but when one of the numerous cameras on board the train was focused on the group from a car window, the party fled precipitately, sharing doubtless the old superstition that a certain portion of one's life is taken to make a portrait. At Elko however, a degenerated chieftain in the attire of civilization was found who expressed a willingness to stand and have his picture taken all day for fifteen cents.

At Palisade, the last place of interest passed before nightfall, some very picturesque scenery is enjoyed, the precipitous rocks on either side being sprinkled with a yellowish moss which resembles copper veining. At this point also a narrow-gauge road diverges to Eureka, where is located the richest gold mine in Nevada. We awake next morning in sight of that strange phenomenon, America's Dead Sea, skirting its borders until we approach Ogden, the terminus of four important railway systems, a city whose beautiful situation we did not have time to inspect as we turn aside here to visit the Mormon Saint's Rest — Salt Lake City.

Perhaps no point in our long journey is regarded with a more curious interest than is the capital of Utah. Its strange history, its religion, built upon only nine commandments of the Decalogue, its long defiance of U. S. laws, with other unusual features increase one's natural desire to see this strange land. In our first drive about the city it was easy to decide that its beauty had been over-rated. We had heard of wide shaded streets with a gently purling river of pure water from the mountains, bordering every curb-stone. We found a swiftly-flowing muddy current in one gutter only of many of the streets, we found wide thoroughfares, it is true, but they were untidy, rough and ill-kept, and the sidewalks were in no cleanlier condition. The trees were almost wholly of the white locust species, which being now in full flower added a needed touch of grace and beauty to the city, which was also bathed in a clear radiant mountain atmosphere imparting a peculiar brilliancy to the sky. A perpetual inspiration is the Wasatch range of snowy peaks, which overlook the city and whose altitude of 13,000 feet it is difficult to realize, being ourselves now nearly 5000 feet above the level of the sea.

Driving first to the Temple enclosure, we visit the Tabernacle, a plain, oblong structure that will seat 8,000, and has twenty double doors of exit. After inspecting its interior, its large organ made of native woods, and testing its hard, uncushioned seats, we ascended to the gallery at the extreme end of the building opposite the pulpit platform (where behind the desk are three or four rows of seats for different orders of the priesthood, and semi-circular accommodation for the Tabernacle choir), and were then treated to an exhibition of the excellent acoustic qualities of the building, a common brass pin when dropped upon a table near the pulpit being distinctly heard over 200 feet away, a whisper was clearly audible, though we strongly suspect this acoustic feat was possible only at that especial angle, or between those two opposite points, for we noticed a disturbing echo when sitting on the side of the sanctuary, and the ceiling was hung with a multitude of very dusty, brown and faded cedar festoons and garlands, placed there on the occasion of a 24th of July celebration, (the anniversary of the Mormon arrival in this place), and these now musty decorations are allowed to still remain because it was found they so greatly improved the acoustic properties of the place.

Within the high stone wall by which this Temple block is surrounded, stands also the Assembly Hall, a handsome structure, used for worship in winter, into which we Gentiles were not admitted, neither gained we entrance to the imposing granite Temple, begun twenty-five years ago and still incomplete, although nearly two millions of dollars have been expended upon it. The streets bounding this Temple block are named East Temple, West, North, and South Temple, the succeeding parallel avenues being First and Second East, or North, a method of designation which leads to many perplexing complications, for when the visiting pedestrian, upon inquiry, is told that he is now at the corner of Fourth South and East Sixth, he begins to lose all interest in localities.

We drove through the main business street where is the Zion's Co-operative Mercantile Institute and other stores, we turned aside into a pleasant avenue which leads to Prospect Hill where a fine view of the city and surrounding country can be obtained, we passed the tithing-house, the Gardo House, which is the Mormon White House, the present incumbent of the presidential office always residing there, we saw the Bee-Hive, the residence of some of Brigham Young's sons, the home where *several* of his widows reside, the small enclosure within the city limits devoted to the prophet's sepulture, and that of his wives, the line of accommodation being drawn at their numerous progeny. One house was pointed out as belonging to a man with two wives and 38 children, whereupon our party began to estimate the number of shoes this patriarch would buy each spring and autumn, multiplied by the number of years of juvenile dependence, but the decimals increased so fast, that the problem became wearisome.

We passed under the Eagle Gate, saw Rose Cottage, the beautiful residence of an English Mormon widow, also the homes of several pensioned wives, as since the recent action of Congress, no Mormon is allowed to visit any save his first wife, under penalty of arrest. Polygamy is now dead, the Endowment House is razed to the ground, property peculiar to their plural rites has been confiscated, but the sad and demoralized fruits of the long reign of error are still painfully apparent. We have never seen such lack of intelligence in human faces, or countenances so utterly devoid of expression of any kind, as on the women and children of this Mormon kingdom. That feminine snap of the eye and carriage of the head common to the woman who has a mind and will of her own and claims the right to its exercise, we did not once discover outside the ranks of their Eastern visitors. We met no Mormon child who was capable of answering a question, though one whom we pleasantly accosted was introduced to our notice by an attendant as "Sadie Cannon, the *fourth* wife's child, you know."

In the afternoon we were treated to an excursion by rail to Salt Lake, 17 miles from the city, stopping at Garfield Beach where a handsome Pavilion has been erected in the water a short distance from the shore, and there are numerous bathing houses. Many of our party improved this opportunity to test a novel experience, that of bathing in water so buoyant that to sink is impossible, the Lake holding 17 per cent of salt, over the 3 or 4 percentage of the Atlantic brine. As the bathing suits provided here are of the brightest hue, the blue waters presented a peculiar kaleidoscopic appearance, as these gayly attired cork dolls floated, bobbed, or writhed in most unusual positions. It is a beautiful Lake, about 80 miles long by 50 wide, with large islands in the near distance, Antelope being 10 miles long and 3000 feet wide. These waters were first navigated by Gen. Fremont in 1842, by Capt. Stansbury in 1850 whose name is given to one of the islands. Numerous fresh water streams pour constantly into this strange basin without in the least affecting its saline quality, and the Lake has no visible outlet. It supports no life save a tiny shrimp or insect, not so large as a New Jersey mosquito. The surrounding sterile-looking shores abound in new and beautiful wild-flowers.

It was with the greatest interest that we sought the Mormon Tabernacle on Sunday afternoon to attend its service, although (perhaps to our shame) the spirit of universal brotherhood sank as low in our soul's barometer as it did in Chinatown, albeit we resolutely looked only for that which was good and commendable, realizing that a spirit of criticism should find no place in any house devoted to praise and worship of the Infinite One. The observance of the Sacrament is a feature of every service, bread and water being passed in silver cake-baskets and flagons from hand to hand, we likewise assisting, though the rite is not observed in silence, for as the deacons and their assistants pass through the vast audience, the delivery of the sermon still goes on. The speakers alternate each Sabbath, an elder being chosen from the various districts in turn. Prof. Talmadge whom it was our chance to hear, is a young and very smart man, but for his morbid religious bias. He ranted a little, and even accused the U. S. government of arraigning itself against the *only* church of Christ, but in a Christian spirit exhorted his hearers to show their worth by their submission and obedience, making the pertinent suggestion that perhaps they had not so far outgrown the remembrance of the persecutions and sufferings of Nauvoo to be entrusted with power which might lead to a desire for revenge. He asserted that if the U. S. government knew what it was doing it would desist, as the hand of the Lord had always been extended to protect this church in every danger that threatened her.

Much of the discourse was lost, or overpowered by the superior lung capacity of hungry and uncomfortable children whose wails were unrestrained. What is the use of acoustic excellence in a building when it is filled with such a large proportion of " Utah's best crop " who squall and lunch by turns? The habit of attendance on religious worship is one early inculcated evidently by the Mormon church. The singing was excellent, the responsive anthem carrying us back to Peace Jubilee days.

Salt Lake City at present is having a boom. The Gentile immigration is very large, the streets are thronged, the city's unattractive hotels are crowded, and there is a spirit of prophecy in the air that Mormonism is on the wane, its record a memory of the past, and not a power of the future.

CHAPTER XXII

THE SCENIC ROUTE

REFRESHED by this break in our journey, glad to have had this opportunity, yet inwardly resolving never to visit Salt Lake City again, on Monday morning we gladly start onward, though we do not immediately leave Mormondom behind, for all through the valley of the river Jordan, (which strangely enough runs into this salt Dead Sea from the fresh Utah Lake, which corresponds in the devout minds of the Latter Day Saint to the Sea of Tiberius, making of this locality a veritable Zion intended for his occupancy), we pass through many Mormon settlements and see plentiful proof, not of miraculous divine intervention, but that clear pluck and faithful toil have coaxed these waste places to laugh into harvests and to blossom as the rose. The Jordan is a muddy, unlovely stream, not so wide but that we could cast a stone to its farther bank.

We have entered upon the course of the Denver and Rio Grande R.R., known as the grandest scenic line in the world, and it wears these laurels deservedly, although to enjoy this wonderful panoramic display the tourist (until the wide track now building, is completed) has to exchange his commodious section, or private drawing-room in a palace-car for the less comfortable, inconvenient narrow-gauge sleepers, whose upper berth is placed so near the ceiling that it is suggestive of nothing else than the top-drawer of a receiving tomb, while the motion of the car at this altitude is something like that which is used in the manufacture of egg-nog. And still the rich experience of the next three days amply repays every discomfort. For how many years, when such possibility seemed a Utopian dream, have we longed to view the grandeur of the Rocky mountains, the backbone of our continent, how often in fancy have we penetrated their wild defiles and mighty cañons, or climbed their stupendous heights; and now this coveted opportunity is ours to enjoy; we are to taste the pleasant fruit which we have craved, indeed without fatigue or effort, it drops into our grasp.

After leaving the valley of the Jordan, we follow Spanish Fork to a pass in the Wasatch range known as Soldier Summit, and soon approach the gateway to this gigantic land, a veritable Castle Gate, two massive buttressed pillars advancing from the cliffs to hold watch and ward before these sacred precincts, not exactly opposite each other though apparently so as we approach them, and our "special" train stops here to do them reverence. We alight and gaze in wonder upon their geometrical proportions and rich coloring, these isolated heights seeming still more impressive as we leave them in the distance, for they appear to draw nearer to each other, after having so charily allowed us room to pass. We now enter upon Castle Cañon, a marvellous region where are the Book Cliffs, so-called perhaps because the ridges of parti-colored rocks lie in even layers, like the successive leaves of a book. But such wonderful fantastic shapes no book ever assumed. Would we could read their ancient record, so boldly written in hieroglyphic cypher, for surely some Titan horde once occupied these lordly castles and kept watch for coming foe from these sightly towers. How impregnable are their fortifications! Note that palace in ruins, how grand its proportions, how extensive its surrounding walls! *Resemblances* to such structures we have seen in rock formations many times before, but surely no semblance these. They are too evidently the work of man, the citadels of a race of giants. And the rich veining of color which is such a feature of this entire region, is here at its height, exciting constant outbursts of glorious surprise. Later on, the cliffs which for several miles have towered near our windows, recede some distance where we view them less minutely but in more extended range, which gives the effect of fair cities whose domes and turrets, and battlements reflect on their red outlines the glow of the setting sun. Ah! if we could preserve forever a vivid picture of this scene, so that we could shut our eyes at any time and still behold it. If it might never grow dim or be crowded from our consciousness. We grow almost jealous of the glory to-morrow holds, which may efface from our fleeting memories the transcendent message of to-day.

From Green River, which we leave at dark, we enter upon a barren uninteresting territory which we are glad to pass over during sleeping hours. We awake on the Uncompahgre Plateau and after breakfast at Cimarron Creek we take the roofless observation-car to better enjoy one of the most soul-inspiring rides the world affords, a run of several miles through the Black Cañon of the Gunnison. Who can describe this mighty gorge? Our wildest conception of its solemn grandeur, its stern features, which the secluded light serves to heighten, is eclipsed by this massive reality. Even our recent experience in the Yo Semite cannot dull the edge of our amazement and delight. Far from it. This sublime cañon cannot suffer by comparison with any other of Nature's masterpieces. It is true the Yo Semite walls rise a thousand or two feet higher than these, but this chasm is so much narrower that the effect of height is even greater. The human eye does not measure rods and roods with accuracy when the scale is elevated skyward. Then again the Yo Semite granite is of pale uniform gray. These giant ledges present such variegated strata, so many brilliant effects contrast with the sombre dark surface, alternating with grandeur of outline, peak behind peak, separated by jagged intersecting cañons, far above our capacity to discern from this lowly road-bed unless we had eyes in the top of our heads; for the hinge in our neck proves inadequate to the excruciating demand upon it. But a beautiful object to admire on our own level is the impetuous sea-green Gunnison river, which rushes noisily by our side, exhibiting strong marks of impatience and dissatisfaction with the limits of its narrow confines.

While still in the depth of the Cañon, a peculiar obelisk arises on the farther side of the river bank which we recognize as the Currecanti Needle, and here we are allowed to alight, and gather vari-colored rocks for souvenirs, while our special artists (all of them) photograph the Needle, and other imposing features of these encircling walls. As we move on, we gain fleeting glimpses of cascades that leap down the mountain sides, one of especial beauty bearing the name of Chipeta falls in honor of the wife of Ouray, a chieftain of the Ute tribe, who was friendly to the early settlers.

We reach Gunnison at noon, realizing for the first time that we are now in Colorado, an enchanted land, of which Joaquin Miller writes: "Colorado, rare Colorado! Yonder she rests; her head of gold pillowed on the Rocky mountains, her feet in the brown grass, the boundless plains for a play-ground; she is set on a hill before the world and the air is very clear so that all may see her well." We seek one of her highest pillows this afternoon. Although quite surfeited with grandeur and would fain defer another feast, we now approach the main range of the Rockies and are to mount and cross the lofty summit known as Marshall Pass, so called because its former toll-man bore that name. Our train is divided into two sections which then proceed to chase each other up one winding stair after another (by a grade 211 feet in a mile), often losing sight of each other in some of the sharp bewildering curves of the mountain's breast, but soon revealed by the black breath and ambitious snortings of our iron steeds, who with sonorous pantings and hollow groans sturdily push their way upward over still steeper grades, along deeper wilder precipices (a most exciting experience), making a dash through an occasional snowshed, until at last the Summit is reached and we look down upon other summits, or hob-nob with loftier peaks across the way, realizing now what the aeronaut's experience must be, or how the world looks over the rim of a balloon. And a very grand beautiful world it is.

We pause at this altitude of over two miles above the sea, where some of our frisky ones engage in a snowballing match with the handsome brakeman, who easily whips the whole crowd, or drives them to the shelter of glass windows. Others of the party remembering that people on mountain heights are frequently scant of breath, anticipating in advance the possibility of being themselves similarly affected, watching narrowly as they near the height, to see how they feel now, really affect the regularity of the heart's pulsation. No organ responds more quickly to the slightest mental excitement and anxiety, on *any* level, but life has its centre and its source in far other altitudes than that compassed by physical elevation, or mundane topography. And if born a little above the level of the fishes, why should it seriously affect us to get so far away from the sea? We live always as spirits in a world of spirit, and the more we realize this, the greater freedom do we enjoy from the dominion of time-worn prejudices, fears and beliefs.

The descent of this grand mountain is very beautiful, so zig-zag in its course that two and three tiers of track are always visible, the severed halves of our train from opposite sides of a cañon, going frequently in different directions, fluttering a shower of white handkerchiefs in friendly greeting. At Salida, a bustling little town we spend the night, with the roar of the swiftly-flowing Arkansas as lullaby. This stop is necessary that we may not lose in the darkness our next scenic display, the Royal Gorge, the further extremity of the Grand Cañon of the Arkansas bearing this title, and right royal it is. Not a third as long as the Black Cañon, the tension upon the beholder's power to absorb is less prolonged, and yet its perpendicular walls and minarets measure a greater height, and so much more obstreperous and grasping is the Arkansas river than the Gunnison, that it grudges even the narrow shelf we have been hitherto glad to accept, or force from the overhanging rocks for our passage, for in one place a hanging bridge, parallel with the stream, has been suspended from an iron framework forged into the ledges which form opposing walls of this Grand Cañon, a triumph of railway engineering. Here too we alight, but a few gasps of admiration are all of which our over full souls are now capable ; we have already enjoyed too much for fitting appreciation of this grand scene. We have overloaded our mental stomachs, and digestion is thereby impaired.

Emerging from our last mountain pass, we see

at Cañon City the guarded walls of the State Penitentiary, and speed on to Pueblo, from whence our track for a time lies between the Fort Scott and Gulf R. R. and the Atchison, Topeka and Santa Fé, the line upon whose rails we skirted this country when bound westward. Since then what rare experience has been ours; one that forms an abiding treasure, to be enshrined in our heart of hearts forever. We make a quick run to Colorado Springs, a place of especial charm (though possessing no springs), with glorious views surrounding it, with Pike's Peak, draped always with ermine far down his royal shoulders, as a perpetual magnet for every aspiring eye. On a sidetrack, six miles away, is Manitou, a romantic little hamlet among the mountains, and it can never become a very large one. The heights do not recede far enough, the prongs by which the eternal hills brace themselves extend almost within the village streets, but what charm does this expression of the "Great Spirit" wear, to what wonders does it hold the key. How grateful is the sweet calm that broods above it, how refreshing this pure, rarified air, how gladly we exchange the restricted confines of our narrow-gauge cars for a whole room, a real bed, a trunk full of untravelled-stained garments, and a blessed three days' rest.

CHAPTER XXIII

HOW WE SPENT MEMORIAL DAY

THE display of festooned bunting over the veranda of the Cliff House, in the early morning, was not a necessary reminder of the tender associations connected with the day, for already, thought had flown to a dear grassy mound far away which we would gladly have crowned with fairest flowers had such rite been essential to express the heart's true remembrance, but happily, neither time nor distance, nay, not death itself can separate soul from soul, or prove a barrier to interchange of loving faithful thought.

We had been treated to a mountain thunder shower the previous afternoon of several hours' duration with hail, and wind, and general blackness, save on Pike's Peak's hoary summit, where a dense snow storm raged. This temporary confinement within doors had so abridged our hours for sight-seeing that visits to several points of interest must be crowded into this charming day. We first walked through the town and inspected its tempting little stores, where are displayed the wealth of the

Rockies, their ores, agates, crystals and gems, wrought into most attractive shapes and designs for souvenirs, or gifts to friends at home, a bewildering array, from which any eye not color-blind must have to turn away, to resist its fascinations. At the Pavilion, near the Cliff House is an especially large collection, and here also are the Manitou and Navajo mineral springs with near by the soda and mineral baths, which some find so refreshing. A short mile away are the famous iron mineral springs, of varied properties and a champagne-like effervescence.

At eight A.M. we start on our first drive in a three-seated carriage, as comfortable as any easy chair in a lady's parlor, taking the trail up through Ute Pass, this being the route used by the Ute tribe of Indians in going to and from their reservation. A short distance after passing the Rainbow falls, our path leaves the road and begins to climb the steep height which rises on our right, a sharp incline which affords us, as we ascend, some beautiful mountain views, and makes us acquainted with two heathen deities, Gog and Magog, or with two pinnacles of rocks thus christened. Before we are aware we have reached the mouth of the Grand Caverns, one of Manitou's notable "lions."

There is always an element of the weird and supernatural about a cave to creatures formed to live in the air and sunshine. To the timid occurs the natural uneasiness lest the entrance hole close up behind them, or the guide lose his way, the weight of darkness oppresses them, the remembrance of those appalling tons of granite that intervene between them and the mountain's summit, while others feel a potent fascination, an irresistible desire to go on and on, to explore each narrow passage way, to delve still deeper into the bowels of the earth. A little distance goes a great way under ground; a few feet are easily stretched, when measured by new sensations, into half a mile. These Grand Caverns were accidentally discovered in 1881, by Mr. George W. Snider, while tracking a deer which here unaccountably disappeared. Four years later, after the cave had been thoroughly explored and cleaned of loose stones and débris, he opened it to the public. Though not extensive, it is an interesting cave and one of the roomiest, safest, the least uncanny and pokerish of any cave we ever visited. It is divided into three sections, the entrance to each one beginning near the outer world, so that visitors can end their explorations at any time.

Equipped with lanterns we follow our guide through Canopy Avenue to Alabaster and Stalactite Halls, our footing dry, the temperature warm and pleasant, the avenues wide with one exception, where the narrow tortuous corridor is named appropriately the Denver and Rio Grande, which includes on its route a Jail and a Bridal Chamber; (no comparisons need be drawn, as the two excavations in this instance are situated widely apart). The Bridal Chamber is the finest room in the cave, though the descent leading to it is steep, slippery and difficult. But here are wondrous formations and we catch the process of their growth, stalactites being seen bearing a tiny glistening drop which has trickled through this rocky ceiling from some unseen spring above us. Near by is a whole waterfall apparently crystallized, or congealed while still flowing. Animals' heads and other realistic shapes abound, a flock of snowy sheep are grazing near, and as fitting climax to this rural scene a large old-fashioned churn is seen with dasher complete.

But the greatest wonder of the whole cave is its natural Organ. The largest chamber is known as the Opera House, a lofty concert hall with two well defined galleries in its upper recesses which our lanterns dimly reveal, and somewhere in the darkness beyond, a torch and a voice discovers the presence of a man in the upper loft who calls our attention to a group of long, curving ribbon stalactites, on which has been discovered a musical scale, slightly flattened in its lower register, but clear in its upper notes, and truly remarkable in every way. The organist, striking with two little sticks at different points upon the suspended stalactites played several tunes, responding graciously to encores from his enthusiastic audience in the pit. Cauliflower and lily pads seemed to grow out of the rocky floor at our feet, and the only piece of artificiality in this natural wonder was a monument to Gen. Grant formed of loose stones, begun on the day of his funeral and now completed.

It is customary in connection with a visit to the Grand Caverns to walk over to the lovely Cave of the Winds, situated on the other side of the same height, but we postponed this pleasure that we might devote more time to the Garden of the Gods, three or four miles distant. This wonderful spot is not happily named. A garden implies culture; this large tract retains its own simple grandeur, untrammelled and unvexed by the hand of improvement. It might once have served as Council Chamber of some primeval deities, whose ruined abbeys and cathedrals spires remain to excite our admiration. The play-ground of tricksy fairies must have been close by, as these red sandstone exclamation points on the face of nature have assumed the most grotesque shapes, which space fails us to enumerate. Even such steady going animals as bears and seals here indulge in a game of peek-a-boo! The entrance to this strange territory is fitly called Mushroom Park, as the rocks standing here have the effrontery to take on the ephemeral shape of toad-stools, which no rock with correct ideas of propriety would think of doing, especially as they are taller than the shrubs which grow around them. Just here we pass the huge balanced rock on its meagre pivotal base and the deer's head so clearly outlined on the opposite side of the narrow passage. But the grandest feature of the place is the colossal gateway with its lonely sentinel always on guard. Through these magnificent portals we gain from the other side an enchanting view of Pike's Peak beyond, contrasting so exquisitely in its graceful slope with these abrupt perpendicular bulwarks, as also its lovely white sheen in the noonday glare, with its canopy of tenderest blue, intensifies the deep red of the cliffs and the rich green of the surrounding foliage. The scene is almost beyond any fiction which imagination might paint. At the base of these red cliffs is a white gypsum bed where material is obtained for the manufacture of the pretty white spar ornaments. "Rare Colorado" indeed! Such a wondrous land as it is, so diverse in its manifestations, so fertile in resources.

A mile or more beyond this point is the beautiful residence and grounds of Gen. Palmer, the father of the Denver and Rio Grande R. R., where these strange formations also abound. It is called Glen Eyrie because an eagle chose to build his nest on the high ledge of an overhanging cliff, occupying it until some miscreant last summer shot the noble bird.

The trip to Cheyenne Cañon and mountain, on whose summit was buried the form of Helen Hunt Jackson, usually consumes a whole day, as a road on the farther side of the mount winds nearly to its apex, but if only a half-day can be devoted to this drive, then a steep and almost impossible climb is necessary to reach the height. Not deterred thereby, on returning from our morning excursion at twelve, we start again at one, for the peak which forms a prominent feature of the landscape for miles around. Passing through Colorado City, the oldest town in the state, and its first capital, where an effort is now being made to locate the State Soldiers' Home, we diverge from Colorado Springs, whose lovely precincts, parks and broad shaded streets we enter later, and soon reach the woody pass which leads to the Cheyenne foot-trail, of the South Cañon.

Alighting here, three determined damsels of the persistent, resolute type (they were not grown in Salt Lake City) set forth in the face of a threatened shower to climb the rugged path. The distance is called a mile and a half, but the Yo Semite scale of measurement is evidently used here. For a long three-quarters of a mile the road is one which it is a luxury to tread, running beside and frequently crossing a beautiful mountain brook, which splashes over its pebbles and babbles sociably in our ears, while our eyes are directed elsewhere, to the steep gray walls that rise so high on either hand that we feel a little as if we had been dropped into a well. We wish it were not necessary to hurry through this majestic aisle, that we could linger here, a suggestion freely offered as advisable by discouraged returning parties who warn us to attempt no higher level, for the ascent is impossible. We leave these faint-hearted ones behind and press on, until, as the walls of the cañon seem to close across our path, we turn a rocky corner and are instantly ushered into the glorious presence of the Seven Falls, one above the other, climbing to a point so much higher than our present low station can trace that we can readily believe the topmost fount must be the hand of Jupiter Pluvius himself. But even the lowest one is alone well worth coming so far to see. It is such an original fall, it leaps in so many different directions, carves out successive stairs for itself, throws its spray so far from these rocky shelves, and it makes such a noise about it that conversation is impossible while we stand on the slender little bridge at its feet.

Leading up to this chasm which the Falls leap down, a narrow wooden stairway has been affixed to the side of the mountain's breast, directly over the rushing torrent, a dizzy-looking cobwebby affair, but nothing daunted we begin the ascent, passing almost through the spray of these successive cataracts, getting nearer and nearer the clouds, over 300 of these ladder rounds being mounted, till we reach the point where the steepest climbing begins. It is on this level that Helen Hunt's summer cottage was erected. Here we meet several sturdy masculine trampers who warn us to "try not the pass," reporting "the toughest climbing ever attempted," it "did not pay," it was "a mile further," with other kindly advice, and to reënforce their suggestions the black cloud which had been hovering above us threatened a drenching, but the gently descending drops proved grateful to our heated faces, and it soon passed over. "Excelsior" was the motto of the undaunted three, and onward and upward they pressed. The face of the mountain here is very nearly perpendicular, a stable foothold being almost impossible to secure. Like the historic frog getting out of the well, progress backward is often more rapid than the ascent gained. A bush to which we can cling occurs only semi-occasionally but in one place of especial difficulty, a short stair is placed, with a chain as handrail. Stopping here to look about us, we note what an exhilarating tonic is this pure mountain ether. A moment or two restores the pristine freshness with which we started.

At last, after one of the steepest grades, **we** clamber over the mountain's brow and stand erect on its summit, whence a level winding path conducts us to the oblong pile of stones under which rests the dust of one unknown in mortal expression, but spiritually dear to all.

> "O soul of fire within a woman's clay!
> Lifting with slender hands a race's wrong,
> Whose mute appeal hushed all thine early song,
> And taught thy passionate heart the loftier way,—
> What shall thy place be in the realm of day?
> What disembodied world can hold thee long,
> Binding thy turbulent pulse with spell more strong?"

A few faded garlands lay upon the cairn, to which we tenderly and reverently added, as our Memorial Day offering, a few wild roses and mulberry blossoms picked by the toilsome wayside. But how sadly we noted the desecration by the autograph fiend of this sacred place. Even upon the small pine tree in whose bark was cut the simple "H. H.", other insignificant initials crowd it too closely. The memorial stones upon the grave are used to hold down the fluttering autographs and pencilled sentimentality of unknown visitors, while surmounting the pile, an unsightly worm-eaten slab of wood is placed to bear the inscription of an entire family. Is there no reverence in the American mind, no idea of the eternal fitness of things? If this prominence of the personality could only be suppressed, this undue assertion of the self-hood. Could there be no lesson learned here of loftier principle, of unselfish devotion to the interests of others, as exemplified in this faithful worker's life, that while standing here could make of this privilege a future inspiration for nobler effort in humanity's service? If one's name might be inscribed in the grateful heart of the lowliest brother, what in comparison this paltry scar upon the face of notoriety? And why need this desecration remain? Is there no one near who loves this dear lady, with authority to remove these disgraceful features?

The spot is beautiful, the view therefrom wonderfully grand. We look *down* the Cheyenne Seven Falls now, we look over and into Colorado Springs and the mountain range beyond. This grand summit must have lent inspiration to the authoress who it is said often used to come here to write, and therefore expressed the wish that this might be her burial place. We may never stand here again, and do not care to, but we know through the law of sympathy and love, that as we aspire upward, even as we have surmounted this difficult height, we shall one day behold the face of this true worker, fair, shining as the sun.

CHAPTER XXIV

THE HOME STRETCH

WE were to leave Manitou for Denver on the morrow, and as we sought our pillows after our over-full day and reviewed all that we had enjoyed in this delightful place, only one regret assailed us; the Cave of the Winds remained unvisited, as well as the charming little Williams' Cañon leading to it through serpentine walls of rock. But might we not still accomplish the latter, although the hour of our departure was an early one, and the entrance to the Cave a mile and a half away? Of course it would not be open, but we could at least see its location. Therefore, after the refreshing oblivion which visits one in these mountain retreats, we shook off the fetters of Morpheus before the sun had left his bed, we emerged into a world not yet awake, and with keenest delight immediately lost ourselves in the winding curves, and ins and outs of this picturesque pass, the walls converging so closely in places that a carriage has barely room to pass, the peaks seeming almost to meet overhead.

Was ever before such morning walk enjoyed? The shadows of the night had so recently lifted from these deep recesses that they seemed freshly created, the tinted pillars and cornices that stand out so boldly from these cavernous cliffs show a heightened color, a richer pink and cream and vermilion, from their fresh bath in mountain dew. Even the air is azure-tinted, an atmosphere that does not wait to be inhaled, but seems to breathe itself into and through each pore and fibre of our being. What an hour of rapture; what a constant study of form and color! What excitement to thread just one more of the many curves in our road, to see what lies beyond it.

When a mile is passed we reach unexpectedly a little house on a bank above the road — any human habitation looking so incongruous in these wild surroundings — where it seems the guide to the Cave we sought keeps old bachelor's hall. This gentleman had just arisen as we passed, and thinking we might wish to visit the natural wonder under his charge, and would be disappointed to find its barriers closed, quietly slipped his untasted breakfast into a basket and followed us with the kind offer, which went straight to our hearts, to open the cavern in advance of usual hours, for our especial benefit, although we learned he would reap no financial benefit thereby, his salary being assured in any case. How many would thus have sacrificed personal comfort and convenience for strangers in whom he had no interest and would never see again? Evidently the law of kindness and unselfishness is fostered in this region.

We chatted along this beautiful cañon for another half-mile when, a little to our dismay, we arrived opposite to the entrance of the Cave, but we were on terra firma, the cavern's mouth was half way to heaven, being situated in the perpendicular face of the cliff, over 300 feet above us. Steep trails alternating with flights of stairs led upward, but would we have time to ascend before the breakfast hour? We resolved to attempt it, remembering we could eat when Manitou and its glories were left behind.

We found this Cave of the Winds a diamond edition, gilt-edged and illustrated, of all the caves it has been our fortune to examine, not that it is smaller than any other, but so choice and exquisite in its minute details. Quaint little stairways lead from one elevation to another and crooked by-paths turn abruptly in an unexpected direction. Its architecture is intricate and copyrighted. We could not visit all of its thirty or more chambers, our time being necessarily so limited, but the excavation known as Dante's Inferno deserves especial mention for the little imps and satyrs of Satanic suggestion are as delicate as an ivory carving. The vegetable garden near by is a fruitful one, abounding in carrots, turnips, beets, and sweet potatoes natural enough to eat. One aisle of exceeding beauty was encrusted on its ceiling and sides with exquisite coral fret-work and floral crystallizations whose finely cut petals our kindly guide revealed more distinctly by a magnesium light. Strange trick of nature to expend such lavish workmanship within this dark recess, hidden so long from every eye. Our chaperon will never know what a rare pleasure he conferred upon us, or how deeply we appreciate it, and as we can never return such favor to him, we will pass it on to his neighbor at every opportunity.

The motto on Denver's escutcheon should read "Thrift, thrift, Horatio!" for this spirit of business enterprise, of energetic push permeates the very air. It is a wonderful city when one remembers its rapid growth, its present wealth and prosperity. Yet nowhere is there any evidence of hasty formation, there is no sham veneering. Great attention has been devoted to the building of substantial structures, Denver profiting perhaps by the lessons wide-spread conflagrations in sister cities have taught her. Even the beautiful dwellings and villas are all of brick or stone, a wooden house of any description being difficult to find. Denver's Court House and the Capitol, now in process of erection, are among the finest buildings in the country. The Trinity (M. E.) church, the largest house of worship, is a beautiful edifice, it has a magnificent organ and possesses also the innovation of private boxes on the gallery floor, which theatrical suggestion grates a little unpleasantly when seen in a house of worship until we learn they are intended for the use of invalids, who can thus recline while listening to the sermon. Fine residences creep out on to the prairie almost outside the city limits, surrounded by green lawns, with the occasional addition of a snow-ball bush, this shrub seeming to comprise Denver's sole floricultural idea. It is a flowerless city and seems especially so with California's gardens still in mind, but remembering the effort of which even the lawns are the fruit, recalling from what sterile soil the place has been so recently evolved, we wait confidently for the next chapter in the city's reeord, when art and adornment receive the same attention given to commercial prosperity.

The second day of our stay in Denver is devoted to a trip to Silver Plume including a descent if desired into the mine, a dark, damp, drippy, disagreeable place where silver is not lying around loose as some had supposed, though veinings of the ore are shown. Lunch is partaken at Georgetown, a pretty place not quite above the clouds, and the mountain scenery which surrounds it, as well as the entire ride through Clear Creek Cañon, where the track makes a complete loop and parallels itself many times, is among the grandest yet enjoyed.

This detour is our last, and for the first time we feel as if we had started for home. We spend the entire next day crossing the broad verdant prairies of Nebraska, reaching Omaha at sunset and its sister city on the hither side of the Missouri — Council Bluffs — a few moments later. Iowa is not skirted in darkness, for we chance to encounter a severe electric storm, which happened to be travelling in the same direction we were taking, and so kept us company the entire night, with incessant flashes, the roar of heaven's artillery, and the patter of descending torrents upon the car-roof. The goblins of the air were all abroad in wildest mood that night. We were glad to be a passenger rather than the engineer, whose exceeding vigilance and caution we could plainly sense as he *felt* his way onward. We heard on the morrow of several narrow escapes; the express train following us had encroached a little too closely on our time, a cloud burst washed away a long stretch of track which we had just passed over, but the providence which never faileth justified our perfect trust in its protection.

The sight of the broad bosom of the Father of

Waters when the radiant morning dawned, moved our party to sing

> "One wide river,
> One more river to cross,"

and recalled the child's query why the *Father* of Waters should not be called Mister-sippi. Soon, with surprise we note how like New England becomes the type of scenery in Illinois. Even the embankments beside the road bristle with wild columbine and have shady groves for background. We are speeding now as the comet flies, approaching Chicago no nearer than Blue Island Junction, dashing across a section of Indiana, losing Michigan and most of Canada in the night, and pausing only to take breath for a long day at Niagara.

Will this marvel of the world seem disappointing to us, we wonder, do we remember it correctly, will it have shrunken in comparison with the grandeur we have recently witnessed? Ah no! Niagara is forever a fresh surprise, it is like nothing else but its own marvellous, stupendous self. A recent storm has muddied the Falls and only the sharpest curve of the horse-shoe bend retains that shimmering, translucent, impossible green. The river will work itself clear again in a day or two; meanwhile it gave new effects of lace fret-work and sparkling frost-like garniture over the contrasting foam-beaten brown. The immense, incredible volume of water that pours over this irregular brink can only be appreciated from the river's lower floor, or at the slight elevation provided by the little steamer Maid of the Mist, which at a safe distance allows the visitor, clad in water-proof garments, to view the marvellous spectacle. To think of a Republic that contains a Niagara, a Yo Semite, and a California! God bless her!

Our last night *en route* is bounded by Buffalo and North Adams. Only three hours lie between us and Boston, only the insignificant little state of Massachusetts to cross, her longest way, to be sure, but such a trifle in comparison with the continent. But where have we seen a fairer state, where lovelier rural scenes in this rarest month of all the year—fresh, leafy June? Graceful New England elms are swaying green pennons across village streets, brooding over time-honored homesteads, or shading pleasant door-yards; broad, generous barns hold the stored wealth of these fertile farms; white spired churches point heavenward, surrounded by plentiful little graveyards (so seldom seen in newer countries); soon we reach the Deerfield river; the broad Connecticut; modest Wachusett, home-like and dear, though humble; lovely woods in sprucest foliage with brand new floor-cloth of curling ferns and violets blue; how beautiful it all is, how rapidly the revolving wheels carry us nearer, still nearer home.

And now the "Home agains" and "Home, sweet homes" have all been sung, the good byes and friendly wishes have been exchanged, for dear old Boston is in sight and excitement reigns. How unchanged it seems; how unconscious it looks of our long absence or the importance of our return. We begrudge the customary pause at the draw-bridge, while we devour the familiar piers, the ships that are imprisoned here, we look over to other bridges that span this tidal Charles, and ride on towards the Fitchburg's wide open doors, pass under its octagonal grey towers, and like John Gilpin,

> "Nor stop till where we did get up
> We do again get down."

The same irregular crooked streets, the same narrow pavements where we jostle everybody's elbows, and try to go *both* sides of the people we meet. But bless us, how clean they all are! What immaculate linen; what spotless *mouchoirs!* The company we have kept for the last day or two has prepared us for nothing like this. The Raymond *lingerie* must be a little off-color.

But how sincerely we pity the people who have not been to California. We often wonder that those who travel habitually turn always to the Old world, before gaining any acquaintance with the New; why cross a stormy ocean, a boisterous channel, and foreign countries by rail and diligence to see — Mount Blanc, for instance, when there are wonderful Alps and Apennines at our own doors waiting to be interviewed; and where in all Europe are there waterfalls to be compared with our own beautiful cataracts and cascades? Then there are the stay-at-home people who can afford to travel and do not, those who are satisfied that their own little hamlet is a good enough place to live in; to such we would respectfully suggest that they can never view their own surroundings correctly until the same are seen through the prospective of distance. Only snails and turtles carry their shells on their backs. A word of advice also to those who think they cannot afford such seeming luxury; viz: resolve you *will* travel and that determination will put forces into action which will eventually project the desired result. You become a magnet to attract the opportunity. Meanwhile, economize to this end. Wear last year's hat another season, turn your dresses inside out, upside down — anything for the glory which shall be revealed to you, anything to give your soul this privilege of widening its borders, of building "statelier chambers," enriching its store of present knowledge, and future accumulation of blessed memories. Money invested in that bank never suffers default, it pays perennial interest at compound rates, and saves your sons-in-law the trouble of spending the fruits of your life-long toil.

If you want to be happy, healthy and wise, if you want to polish down the sharp angles of narrow selfish interests or morbid slant, if you want to grow into the image and likeness of the Creator of this beautiful world, which in all its glory is but a shadow of the *real* Home of the Soul, then—travel!